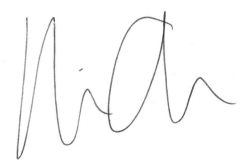

BREAKFAST WITH NICK: COLUMBUS

Your Guide to the Morning Meal
in Ohio's Capitol City
By Nicholas Dekker

ISBN 978-1-4507-9952-2

Printed in the United States
By Old Trail Printing
oldtrailprinting.com

TABLE OF CONTENTS

BREAKFAST WITH NICK   6

BREAKFAST IN COLUMBUS   8

COLUMBUS BREAKFAST MAP   11

NORTHWEST   13
DUBLIN, GRANDVIEW, HILLIARD, POWELL, UPPER ARLINGTON

NORTHEAST   35
BEECHWOLD, EASTON, POLARIS, WESTERVILLE, WORTHINGTON

CENTRAL   53
CAMPUS, CLINTONVILLE, DOWNTOWN, OLD NORTH, SHORT NORTH

SOUTHWEST   81
FRANKLINTON, GROVE CITY, HILLTOP, SOUTH HIGH STREET

SOUTHEAST   99
BEXLEY, EAST SIDE, GAHANNA, GERMAN VILLAGE, OLDE TOWNE EAST

INDEX   116

SPECIAL THANKS   119

ACKNOWLEDGEMENTS   120

BREAKFAST WITH NICK

Hi, I'm Nick, and I love breakfast. People ask me "Why breakfast?" after they read my blog or one of my published articles, or while just watching me pile scrambled eggs on toast. Aside from the obvious reply of "Why not?" my next answer is that it's in my blood.

This book is about Columbus, but before we talk about it, we have to visit my hometown. I'm not a Columbus native. Maybe that's disappointing or somehow disqualifies me from serving as your Columbus breakfast guide. But before you dismiss my credentials, I offer you this: I was born, raised, and educated in Grand Rapids, Michigan, and GR is an amazing breakfast city. Grand Rapidians take their breakfast seriously. Business meeting? Go to Marie Catrib's. College class discussion? Meet up at Wolfgang's. Going out with the family on Saturday? Head to The Omelette Shop. Being from Grand Rapids is akin to putting "professional breakfaster" on your resume.

But why do I really love breakfast? Well...

1. IT'S A START...

I'm one of those insufferable morning people. When I have a day off, I look forward to getting up early. I love a quiet house, a cup of coffee, time to read or write. Ever since I was a kid, I always thrilled at the thought of going to breakfast the following day. I couldn't imagine more exciting words than "Let's go to breakfast tomorrow morning." I loved (and still love) making plans, going out in the morning, and starting the day with a meal in a crowded cafe or diner.

The morning always has so much potential. It's a new day. All of your plans lay before you. The feel of a busy restaurant exemplifies all that is good about the morning. Looking around, you see people holding meetings. Friends reconnecting. Families enjoying a meal together. Going out to breakfast, you get to share in the start of everyone's day, not just your own.

2. IT'S THE PLACE...

Breakfast is an excuse to gather regularly. We love the consistency and familiarity of our own breakfast spot. There are small diners and cafes all around the world - many of them completely unremarkable in terms of food - that are loyally loved and fiercely defended by their clientele. Customers love a place because they have their regular spot at the counter, their own banter with the servers, and their own camaraderie with their fellow diners. They love a place simply because it is theirs.

Photo by David Dekker

My earliest breakfast love was a small restaurant in my hometown called the Boston House. My family often went on Saturday mornings, and you'd see the same people there, at the same times, in the same seats. I could always find Mr. Jager, my high school cross country coach, there with his family. I always ordered the same thing: the BBB, or Big Boston Breakfast. Scrambled eggs, hash browns, sausage links, bacon, and toast. Plus a glass of chocolate milk. I later visited Boston House with college roommates; it was cheap and ideal for the late-risers. One of my professors even occasionally held class there. Nothing like discussing Brechtian theatre techniques over eggs and pancakes. Boston House is now closed, but such is the way with small restaurants. We savor the memories and find a new place to make our own. Today, that hometown love has been replaced by a place simply called the Real Food Café. Real Food exemplifies all that is good about the neighborhood cafe. It's mere blocks from my parents' house. You can find them there around 9 a.m. every Saturday morning. I see old friends, neighbors, and professors there. The servers know you. Owner Frank Amodeo stands behind the counter, making omelets, grilling potatoes, and whipping up the best eggs benedict I've ever tasted. The cafe is bright and colorful, crowded with regulars, and always, always alive with chatter. Whenever we're home visiting, someone says on Friday night, "Real Food in the morning?" All across America, that same conversation takes place: "Shall we go to _____ in the morning?" Just insert the name of your local diner.

3. IT'S THE PEOPLE...

Breakfast is often not a very dynamic meal. Eggs. Bacon. Toast. Coffee. There are only so many ways you can prepare them. What matters more is not what you're eating, but with whom you're eating it. Many greasy eggs and sub par pancakes have been overlooked because the customer is in good company. We forgive our little diners for their mistakes, because we're really there for the people.

When I was younger, my paternal grandfather used to take one of his grandsons to breakfast every Saturday morning. We rotated turns each week; he took us the same time, every Saturday, and always to the same place, although he gave us the illusion of choosing where to go. It was like the Model-T Ford: you could go anywhere you wanted for breakfast, as long as you wanted to go to Arnie's. (One week, I even suggested a different restaurant. Grandpa willingly took me there, sipping on coffee while I ate eggs and toast. When I was finished, he said, "Are you done? Good, let's go to Arnie's.") One of the real reasons he took us there was because he knew *everybody* there. We'd stroll by the

"Being from Grand Rapids is akin to putting "professional breakfaster" on your resume."

booths and hear everyone say, "Hi, Marty!" He'd make chit-chat and introduce his grandson. It was like he owned the place. When he passed away unexpectedly in 1987, my grandmother found his day planner, with the next breakfast penciled in.

All of these things I've described - the time, the place, the people - those are the reasons why I love breakfast. And the great thing about breakfast? You'll find these things no matter where you eat it: Grand Rapids, Columbus, across the country, and around the world.

In June of 2007, I mentioned the idea to my wife of blogging about the great places we had enjoyed breakfast, from the Boston Houses to the Real Food Cafes and beyond. She encouraged me to do it. As I wrote more posts, especially about Columbus, people started e-mailing to ask for recommendations or to suggest new spots. In 2010, the blog drew the attention of Rick Sebak, producer for WQED Pittsburgh. Rick was making a documentary called *Breakfast Special* for PBS, and asked if I could show them around to a couple stops in Columbus. Getting to appear on national television added some legitimacy to the blog, as did getting to write for *(614) Magazine* and other guest blogs. As the momentum built, my wife and I began to discuss creating a full guidebook to breakfast in Columbus. We did our research, and approached our friend Robin Oatts to photograph and design it. She said, yes, and here we are.

BREAKFAST IN COLUMBUS

Now let's talk about the places and people of Columbus.

Columbus is many things. Ohio's capitol city. The largest city in the state. The fifteenth largest in the country. Located in the middle of farmland. Home to a gigantic research university with high profile athletic programs. Full of revitalized historic districts, sprawling suburbs, and a reawakened downtown. With a bustling arts scene, a healthy appetite for sports, and several financial centers. Traditional and progressive. A landlocked Midwestern city named for a fifteenth century Italian explorer.

Breakfast in Columbus is many things as well. It's a perfect crossroads between the traditional and the innovative. You'll find a good dose of history and a healthy sense of exploration. We've got decades-old diners and brand new eateries attempting original recipes.

In this book you'll get a complete look at all of them: old diners, classic brunches, casual cafes, donut joints, coffee shops, and everything in between. Most importantly, you'll get to hear the stories. That's what this book is really about: the stories of entrepreneurs finally opening their dream restaurant. Of families passing down the love of food from generation to generation. Of regulars who became the owners, looking to serve customers as they were once served. Of cooks and chefs desperate to share their national cuisine with their adopted city. It's stories that illustrate the people of Columbus' passion to create a community around food, even food as basic as scrambled eggs and a plate of bacon.

EXPLORING COLUMBUS WITH THIS BOOK

To keep things simple, I've roughly divided Columbus into five sections: the four corners (NW, NE, SW, SE) and a central corridor. I realize that, yes, such divisions are somewhat arbitrary and completely debatable. But they gave us a helpful starting place in structuring the book and organizing Columbus' various neighborhoods, districts, and suburbs.

Within each section, I've featured a handful of restaurants that I think are exemplary for their food, community, and/or history. They provide a good cross section of Columbus' breakfast geographically, stylistically, and ethnically. If you need a quick idea for breakfast, these features are your go-to. There are also little sidebars that offer additional information or suggest short breakfasting trips outside of the city.

Some other reminders as you plan your breakfast or brunch outings around town:

- Hours change, menu items come and go, restaurants open and close. Check the website. Call ahead.
- Eat lunch and dinner, too! There are a lot of fantastic breakfasts around town, but don't forget to patronize these establishments throughout the day as well.
- Tell others about it! Write a blog post, share it on Facebook, brag on Twitter. Whenever possible, we've included Twitter handles to allow you to tell everyone where you're breakfasting and what you think of it (if you're the Twittering type).
- Go with others. Gather the family, call up some friends. Breakfast is always better when you can experience it in community.

Columbus residents and Columbus visitors: I challenge you to explore. Visit a corner of the map you rarely frequent. Try a place you've never heard of before. Experience a breakfast cuisine from a different culture. Share in the pride and community of each neighborhood. Columbus is rich in breakfast culture, and we hope this book is your guide to finding that out-of-the-way diner you never knew existed.

A WORD ON CHAIN RESTAURANTS

Like every good American city, Columbus is peppered with chain restaurants. It's an unavoidable fact. We've all visited them, in town or across the country. They're convenient, they're cheap, and they're recognizable.

That's also the downside. No offense to any of these corporations, but the fact that they dominate highway signage and the fact that they can offer a quick meal for 99 cents means that they've stolen business from some true American treasures. The mom-and-pop, hole-in-the-wall, been-around-for-decades restaurants too often get crowded out. And that's where I'm hoping to step in and show you how to find these little places, so you can rub elbows with the locals, meet the owners, and watch them make you breakfast.

But like it or not, the national and regional chains are part of Columbus' breakfast DNA. I'd be remiss to ignore them completely, so I want to acknowledge who's set up shop in our city.

The biggest fast food chains - *McDonald's, Wendy's, Burger King, Subway,* even Columbus' own *White Castle* - have all jumped on the breakfast bandwagon. McBakedWithSyrup sandwiches, brunch wrap extremes, hotcakes, premium coffee, you name it. You can find these anywhere in Columbus, on every major roadway, off every highway exit.

Some chains are known first and foremost for their donuts. *Tim Horton's*, that Canadian import that we get to taste because they were once owned by Dublin-based Wendy's, does a healthy business of sandwiches and boxes of TimBits. Or *Dunkin' Donuts*, which has been slowly but steadily expanding its Columbus market with donut holes and coffee. And customers from all over gather like bugs to the zapper when that pink neon light goes on at *Krispy Kreme*, announcing the arrival of fresh donuts. These places are known and loved for their reliable donuts, their okay coffee, and their quick-order breakfast sandwiches.

There's a middle class of breakfast chains that offer higher quality food, and often feature coffee and pastries. These are the places like *Panera* and *Cosí*. Panera is known for their gorgeous spread of pastries set before you each day, while *Cosí* does a healthy business of breakfast wraps, square bagels (yes, called Squagels), and oatmeal. We've also got a handful of *Bruegger's Bagels* and *Einstein Bros. Bagels*. Even sandwich chain *Potbelly* has added breakfast sandwiches and oatmeal at select locations.

"That's what this book is really about. It's stories of Columbus' passion to create a community around food, even food as basic as scrambled eggs and a plate of bacon."

Coffee chains abound in Columbus. McDonald's, Panera, and Dunkin' Donuts are edging out the market, with Mickey D's encroaching on *Starbucks'* coffee shop territory. Although the Starbucks corporation has scaled back its expansion overall, you can still find at least one purveyor of your double caramel half-caf macchiato in your neighborhood.

And then there are the sit-down restaurants, the ones that make for relaxing stops while traveling the interstates. For some reason, people go nuts when they see *Cracker Barrel* signs. Maybe it's the big white rocking chairs out front. Perhaps it's the gift shop at the front of the store. Or maybe it's the made-from-scratch recipes. (In college I worked at a car rental agency, and I kid you not, on many occasions customers' first question would

be, "Where's the closest Cracker Barrel?" What?!) If country kitchen isn't your style, you can always go late night greasy diner with *Waffle House*. Their tall yellow signs announce tiny locations huddled next to the highway, serving signature waffles and hash browns. Looking for another late night option? We have one *Perkins* on the west side. Greater Columbus recently got its first *IHOP* since the 1980's, although you have to trek out to Reynoldsburg to try it.

In Ohio, there's one sit-down chain that pops up more than others. It started as a restaurant counter on his farm, serving homemade sausage, and now *Bob Evans* has grown into an Ohio institution. Those familiar red barn structures with the big awnings and yellow lettering pop up all over the Midwest. Columbus alone is host to roughly sixteen of their restaurants. They serve "farm style" breakfasts of eggs, omelets, hotcakes, biscuits and gravy, and of course, sausage. If you want to take your Bob Evans experience one step further, you can trek down to Rio Grande, Ohio, to see the original Bob Evans Farms, where he started making sausage, serving breakfast, and hosting visitors in the 1950's. The 1000-acre farm, recently renovated, still houses "Restaurant #1," as well as a museum and the Homestead, the former home of Bob and Jewel Evans and their children.

There are a few more single-location chains included in the book. These are in the general listings, and will be identified as chains.

Now, let's start exploring...

COLUMBUS BREAKFAST MAP

NORTHWEST
DUBLIN, GRANDVIEW, HILLIARD, POWELL, UPPER ARLINGTON

NORTHEAST
BEECHWOLD, EASTON, POLARIS, WESTERVILLE, WORTHINGTON

CENTRAL
CAMPUS, CLINTONVILLE, DOWNTOWN, OLD NORTH, SHORT NORTH

SOUTHWEST
FRANKLINTON, GROVE CITY, HILLTOP, SOUTH HIGH STREET

SOUTHEAST
BEXLEY, EAST SIDE, GAHANNA, GERMAN VILLAGE, OLDE TOWNE EAST

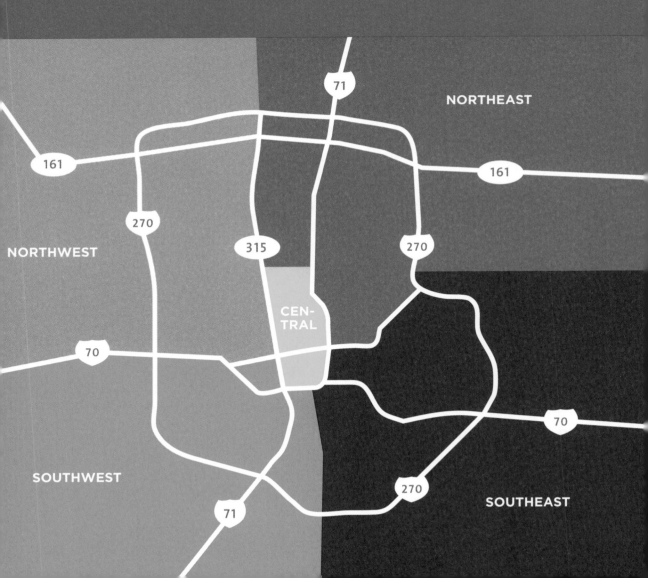

NORTHWEST

GRANDVIEW, UPPER ARLINGTON, HILLIARD, DUBLIN, POWELL

The northwest section of Columbus spans a wide range of neighborhoods, from Grandview, an older suburb northwest of downtown, to the more affluent Upper Arlington and Dublin, to the further reaches like Hilliard and Powell. In this great variety of neighborhoods, you'll find a diverse mix of breakfasts, including some of the best donuts in town, classic diners, elegant tea houses, and a magnificent collection of ethnic eats, from Chinese to Mexican to Vietnamese to Cuban. This part of the city invites you to explore and expand your horizons.

CAMBRIDGE TEA HOUSE

1885 West Fifth Avenue
Columbus, OH 43212

(614) 486-6464

cambridgeteahouse.com

@cambridgethouse

Mary Boesch's story is one of those great tales of the American small business. Mary has a law degree and spent her career in banking, but wanted to explore new adventures and passions later in life. She moved to Columbus to follow her children and grandchildren, and had the idea to open a small bakery. During a six-month stay in New York City with her daughter (Tricia Wheeler, who was studying at the French Culinary Institute and would later become editor of *Edible Columbus*), Mary include anything from cherry chocolate chip to cinnamon spice, and cranberry orange to coconut lime white chocolate. Order your scones with jam or homemade clotted cream. (Although it isn't technically true Devonshire clotted cream, due to differing food regulations between the U.K. and the U.S., Cambridge Tea House's comes amazingly close.)

You can also enjoy tea bread for a simple snack, or more filling dishes like a daily quiche special, rich

"Mary's passion has given Columbus a place to enjoy a quiet and relaxing meal in an intricately decorated and arranged setting."

changed her concept from a bakery to a tearoom after visiting famous teahouses like Alice's Tea Cup, the Carlyle Hotel, and Tea & Sympathy.

She returned to Columbus on weekends to scout locations, eventually finding an historic repurposed building in the Marble Cliff neighborhood, just west of Grandview. The red brick and stone building dates back to the early 1920's and originally served as a gas station. The middle shops, with their tall windows, were once bays for servicing cars. Eat in the dining room of Cambridge Tea House, and you're sitting under the overhang where cars used to pump gas.

Mary chose to serve Harney & Son's tea. Harney's is based in New York, and when doing her research she toured the tasting room in Millterton and met Michael Harney (one of the sons). The tea service she's created at Cambridge Tea House offers tea done properly. Pots of loose leaf tea are served under tea cozies, at the proper temperature, and you're given heated mugs. You can order a wide variety of Harney & Son's teas as well: herbal, green, white, black, oolong, plus flavored versions and seasonal specialties.

To complement the tea, the breakfast menu features lighter dishes. One of the best pairings for your tea are the homemade scones, which are amongst the best in town. Scone flavors vary daily, and can

oatmeal with fruit, egg and cheese sandwiches, housemade granola, blueberry pancakes, or flavored Greek yogurt. The menu changes seasonally with local ingredients, so different specials come and go.

Mary's passion has given Columbus a place to enjoy a quiet and relaxing meal in an intricately decorated and arranged setting. Sip on tea with friends and take in the detailed decorations, the patterned pastoral scenes on the valances, and the delicate windows. Enjoy afternoon tea while you gaze at the tantalizing stack of fresh scones, the hand-written menu above the counter, and the shelves of tea equipment.

CHEF-O-NETTE

2090 Tremont Center
Columbus, OH 43221

(614) 488-8444

chefonette.com

Chef-O-Nette is one of those places where the regulars are always ready to tell you the story of the restaurant. You walk in the door and one immediately reminds you that Chef-O-Nette is America's first drive-through. Another will corner you to explain how they've eaten at Chef-O-Nette since it opened. Even the servers contend to see who's worked there longer. There's Jeanie, at about 23 years. Or Peggy, who's been there over 25.

The McKinley family opened Chef-O-Nette's doors in 1955 in Upper Arlington's Tremont Center. Mrs. McKinley provided the unique name for the restaurant, although she never passed on its origin to subsequent owners, so the true meaning remains a mystery. In 1970, Maborn Howard, who previously ran Miller's Village Inn in Gahanna, purchased Chef-O-Nette from the restaurant's second owners, Jim Reid and Chuck Zollinger; his eleven-year-old son Harlan began working then as a bus-boy. Over the years, Harlan worked his way up from bus-boy to cashier to cook to doing, well, everything; he eventually purchased the restaurant from his father in 1993. Today you can find him trading jokes with customers at the counter or cooking your breakfast in the kitchen.

"Many of its regulars weren't born when it opened. Either that, or it opened around the time they were born."

Regarding the claim of being the first drive-through, Chef-O-Nette has been serving breakfast out the little window since its inception. Sure, there were drive-ins across the country (Columbus' first, Dan's, opened downtown in 1952), but Harlan has yet to find anyone who opened a drive-*through* earlier than his restaurant.

Today, the restaurant is like a museum for the 1950's. Harlan and his crew use a lot of the original equipment. There are formica floors and patterned carpets. Two half circle counters angle out into the space, with openings directly into the kitchen. Red leather swivel stools surround the counters. Walls are decorated with old wood panelling, mirrors, and lattice work. One section is hung with pictures and letters from the community, thanking Harlan and the restaurant for their support of Upper Arlington.

Chef-O-Nette speaks to the longevity of classic breakfast joints. Many of its regulars weren't born when it opened. Either that, or it opened around the time they were born. Regardless of age, generation after generation passes on the tradition of enjoying waffles and pancakes, breakfast sandwiches, and eggs and sausage at the restaurant. Maborn Howard joked with his regulars, and now his son Harlan jokes with their children.

CUCO'S
TAQUERIA

2162 Henderson Road
Columbus, OH 43220

(614) 538-8701

cucostaqueria.com

@cucostaqueria

> **"Cuco is a nickname for Refujio, and a taqueria is a small taco stand, so Cuco's Taqueria refers to Juan's father's business back home."**

Most people know Cuco's Taqueria as one of Columbus' best Mexican restaurants, but did you know that it also serves an amazing breakfast? You can trade your margaritas and salsa bar for an early morning meal of breakfast burritos and eggs with chorizo.

Owner Juan Morales opened the restaurant in July 2003, originally offering counter service and featuring tacos. Over the years he and his family expanded the menu and the restaurant's shape, adding breakfast after about five years. Juan himself has worked around food all his life. The name Cuco's is an acknowledgement of his family's business back in Guadalajara, Jalisco, Mexico. His father Refujio still runs a small food stand there, serving tacos every morning starting at 8 a.m. "Cuco" is a nickname for Refujio, and a taqueria is a small taco stand, so *Cuco's Taqueria* refers to Juan's father's business back home."

The Columbus Cuco's is decorated in the standard style of Mexican restaurants: bright colors, neon advertisements for Corona and Dos Equis, with Spanish-language music blaring over the speakers. The entryway looks like market shelves stocked with hot sauces, cans of black beans, and jugs of mango juice.

A traditional Mexican breakfast might include something like *chilaquiles*, which are tortilla strips sautéed with a verde sauce, then baked with cheese and eggs. You may also find the *machaca*, a spiced shredded beef that's often served with eggs, vegetables, and tortillas. You'll often find these traditional items on the Cuco's breakfast menu, plus a few more additions. The *oaxaqueña*, for instance, includes egg and potato enchiladas, with black

bean sauce, sour cream and lettuce (although the traditional Mexican version uses refried beans rather than black). There are also *moyetes*: a grilled roll topped with chorizo, beans, and cheese.

Juan has adapted the menu at Cuco's to make some concessions to American dining as well. The breakfast burrito, for instance, is a common item

in Mexican restaurants today, although it's a dish that was developed in the U.S. But that shouldn't stop you from feasting on a giant breakfast burrito loaded with eggs, cheese, potatoes, and chorizo. Other American specialties include omelets and French toast, and The Plato Americano features eggs, bacon, and pancakes. Whatever you order, though, you can experience a bit of Juan's and his family's heritage at their restaurant.

DK DINER

1715 West Third Avenue
Columbus, OH 43212

(614) 488-5160

thedkdiner.com

@dkdiner

All you need to know about DK Diner is summed up in that simple opening acronym: "Donut Kitchen."

Just over 20 years ago, the Teny family bought a five-year-old restaurant called the Donut Kitchen, down the street from Grandview High School. They took over the operation, continuing to make the namesake pastries, but mainly using the restaurant as a base for their catering business, Caterers Three. Anthony Teny, who was in high school when his stepfather Stacy took over the Donut Kitchen, learned donut-making at age 16. He began by using the basic recipes in place at the restaurant, and got so familiar with them that, when the scale broke thirteen years ago, they didn't bother replacing it. Now he knows the recipes so well he can simply eyeball the right amounts of water, flour, yeast, and so on.

The family continued making just donuts for the first four years, then added lunch in 1995. Several years later, in the early 2000s, they expanded to include breakfast and renamed the restaurant DK Diner, to let people know they serve more than just donuts.

"Anthony knows the recipes so well he can simply eyeball the right amounts of water, flour, yeast, and so on."

But let's be honest... the donuts are still the mainstay. The display cases at DK are lined with yellow trays full of goodies: softball-sized apple fritters; chocolate and vanilla creme Bismarcks; and rows and rows of cakey sour cream donuts in plain, blueberry, chocolate, and more.

DK still gives you the full diner experience. They produce simple, good quality food, with a focus on serving their immediate neighborhood. Employees and regulars banter back and forth, families gather for

breakfast underneath memoribilia from Grandview-area schools. Ohio State students past and present find a hearty lunch. The customary table of old folks sipping their coffee is full by 10 a.m. Word of mouth has made the diner a popular spot for a quick breakfast or a box of some of Columbus' best donuts.

Favorite breakfast dishes include Dana's Deluxe BS: a Texas toast sandwich piled high with fried eggs, meat, tomatoes, cheese, lettuce, and mayo. The sandwich is named after a woman who worked at the diner, as she made the sandwich for her kids. If you can't choose, there's always the DK All The Way, a platter of eggs, Canadian bacon, potatoes, and biscuits smothered in gravy. Or, if you can't get enough of the donuts, order the pancakes, which are made with DK's vanilla donut mix.

Anthony laughs that DK has become known for their "ugly" donuts. In truth, customers that comment on the slightly misshapen donuts reveal that they are more familiar with assembly-line pastries made by the chain restaurants. Instead, the non-perfect production tells discerning customers that these donuts were lovingly made by hand, *that* morning starting around 4:00 a.m. And besides, the donuts taste right, says Anthony, so why worry about their looks? Most weekdays, he makes anywhere from 15-20 dozen; on Fridays and Saturdays, he puts together 30-40 dozen to keep up with his customers. Donuts are usually ready by 7 a.m.; occasionally they've sold out by 8 a.m.

LAC VIET RESTAURANT

1506 Bethel Road
Columbus, OH 43220

(614) 451-6299

Thang Nguyen is on a mission to teach Columbus about Vietnamese food. Growing up in Saigon, he regularly visited the local market with his mother. When his family moved to Columbus in 1975, they swapped their local Saigon market with downtown's North Market. He was fascinated by the market and dreamed of owning his own stall there, selling Vietnamese food to the masses. In August of 2004, he got his chance, and Lac Viet opened in the northwest corner of the market.

"One of the most well-known staples of Vietnamese cooking is phò, a warm noodle soup that's served at any meal, including breakfast."

Mr. Thang worked for the U.S. Postal Service for 31 years, so he understands the value of building relationships with the people you meet. This made him ideal for his North Market eatery, where regulars quickly grew to know his smiling face and warm welcome. Upon his retirement from the Postal Service in 2010, he moved his restaurant north to Bethel Road. (The North Market stall continues with a different owner under the name Lan Viet.)

With the opening of his Bethel Road restaurant, Mr. Thang added breakfast to his menu, and not just Vietnamese breakfast. Even the standard breakfast offerings are punched up with new ingredients. Oatmeal, for instance, is mixed with seasonal fresh fruit or dried fruits like apricots, dates, raisins, or currants. Omelets can be made with cheese, mushrooms, or vegetables, or even shrimp, smoked jowl, and vegan ham. Breakfast sandwiches are made with fried eggs, ham, pickled radish, cilantro, and paté.

The more traditional Vietnamese breakfast dishes include porridge made with rice, coconut milk, and star anise. The sweet potato hash mixes onions, cumin, and then shrimp, vegan ham, or bacon and eggs. One of the most well known staples of Vietnamese cooking is phò, a warm noodle soup that's served at any meal, including breakfast. Mr. Thang makes the base broth in large batches from scratch; it often takes twelve to fourteen hours to complete. The soup is served with chicken or beef, and garnished with bean sprouts, herbs, and lime.

You can try a fantastic array of drinks, too: Vietnamese coffee made with condensed milk, jasmine or orange flower tea, kumquat juice, or smoothies made with peanut butter, blueberries, strawberries, bananas, and green tea.

Mr. Thang is on a mission to spread breakfast world-wide. Check in to his restaurant to sample their rotating Global Breakfast menu, including sweet sticky rice from southeast Asia to Indian dosas to Spanish specialities. Customers can even vote or suggest different breakfasts from around the world!

STARLINER DINER

5240 Cemetary Road
Hillard, OH 43026

(614) 529-1198

starlinerdiner.com

@starlinerdiner

Starliner Diner is regularly voted one of Columbus' top breakfasts, and rightfully so. It has all the elements of a good diner: it is off the beaten path; the decor is kooky and eclectic; there are long-time servers and kitchen staff who know their customers; and the only problem with the food is that you're conflicted between ordering your regular or a daily special.

Owner Molly Davis started Starliner in late 1994. She and her partner operated the restaurant together: he cooked and she waited tables. Their restaurant was inspired by a now-gone eatery across from the CBS studios in West Hollywood, California, called the Authentic Cafe. They named the diner after the Starliner, an automobile from Ford's Galaxy series. After the diner opened, Molly actually found a 1960 Starliner for sale. You can see pictures of the car on their website. Their inspiration resulted in a colorful little diner, up on a hill in Hilliard next to some train tracks. While you sip coffee, take in the wall full of different clocks. Or look through the row of lamps hanging from the ceiling. Or take in the brightly painted wall with space-themed drawings.

"The only problem with the food is that you're conflicted between ordering your regular or a daily special."

Yes, you can get pancakes, eggs, and toast on the Starliner breakfast menu, but the real treats are the dishes that "come alive," as Molly describes it. The Breakfast Tradicionales features Cuban fare that ranks as some of the most flavorful breakfasts in Columbus. The huevo rancheros, for instance, include eggs served over corn tortillas with cheese, a spiced ranchero sauce full of vegetables, and a bed of black beans or home fries. The chilaquiles are rich with onions, peppers, zucchini, corn,

complemented by eggs, tortilla chips, and black beans. Of course, add the chorizo. A giant bowl of Cuban French toast includes an entire loaf of house-made Cuban bread, cubed, dipped in batter and

fried, then served with fruit. You don't even need the syrup! Other specials like machaca (shredded pork with eggs and veggies) or Mexican chorizo omelets round out an adventurous menu.

Starliner is a short drive out of central Columbus, but if you're one of those eaters who are "young at heart," as Molly says, then a visit to the diner is more than worth it. As are all repeat visits.

SUNFLOWER CHINESE RESTAURANT

7370 Sawmill Road
Columbus, OH 43235

(614) 764-7888

columbussunflower.com

Dining at Sunflower Chinese Restaurant is always a delightfully colorful experience. The crowded entryway is filled with fish tanks; the red and gold decorations throughout the restaurant provide a bright background to your meal. Perhaps the most welcoming sight is owner Danny Chung strolling through the dining room in his signature brightly colored shirts and dark suspenders.

Danny is especially proud that many Chinese families seek out his restaurant for an authentic meal. Growing up in Hong Kong, he immigrated to the United States at age 20 and settled in Philadelphia. He laughs when he tells you how he followed a girlfriend to Columbus, but when they broke up, he was left to his own devices. Over the years, he worked nearly every position in the restaurant industry, until finally in 1996 he was poised to open his own place. He chose the name sunflower for its symbolism in Chinese as "my new flower" or "my first adventure."

Danny's first adventure has made a name serving some of the best dim sum in Columbus. Dim sum is the original brunch. The term is translated literally in

up tableside, select any of the dishes from it and the server marks the card at your table. If there's something you don't recognize, be sure to ask. You'll see wooden baskets with steamed or fried dumplings filled with chicken, shrimp, pork, or vegetables. There are long rice noodles filled with pork and covered with soy sauce. Small trays and plates are filled with

"Danny's first adventure has made a name serving some of the best dim sum in Columbus."

Cantonese as "snack," but broader interpretations have included phrases like "to touch your heart," "a bit of heart," "heart's delight," or "order to the heart's content." Nowadays, dim sum seems to encapsulate all of those concepts, so perhaps we can think of it as a heart-warming small meal. The meal itself originated in the Canton province of China, and is served during what's now considered standard brunch hours, from mid-morning to early afternoon. A key component of the meal is drinking tea, so expect that anywhere you try it. Dim sum made its way to the Western world via Chinese immigrants in the nineteenth century, and its tradition is thought to have created the modern brunch.

Dim sum dishes are wide and varied. The full service is provided through a variety of carts that are pushed around the dining room. When a cart is drawn

other fried or steamed delicacies. Some plates are for the more adventurous, but are worth trying: chicken feet sauteed in a hot peppery sauce, and chicken or pork simmered with bone and cartilage to maximize the flavor. One dish includes chicken, vegetables, rice, and a quail egg wrapped together in a lotus leaf and steamed. Another weaves a crisp, lightly fried basket filled with chicken, cashews, and vegetables.

At Sunflower, you can eat dim sum from a smaller menu at lunch hours, but to get the true experience, you need to visit on the weekends. It's an exemplary meal for its emphasis on community. It's meant to be enjoyed with your family or a group of friends, so if you're looking for an opportunity to draw together, let Danny provide you the space for it.

EXTRA HELPINGS

161 DINER
3670 West Dublin Granville Road
(inside Whole Foods)
Dublin, OH 43235
(614) 760-5556

If brunching while shopping is your thing, you can saddle up at the small diner counter inside Whole Foods Market. They serve brunch only on weekends, but you can try all of your favorites, like pancakes, omelets, waffles, eggs benedict, and stuffed French toast.

ABNER'S CASUAL DINING
4051 Main Street
Hilliard, OH 43026
(614) 876-2649
abnersrestaurant.com

It's quintessential small-town America: Abner's Casual Dining's little storefront can be found on, yes, Main Street in Hilliard. They serve breakfast every morning, allowing customers to feast on Early Riser egg combos, buttermilk or cornmeal pancakes, or ribeye steak and eggs.

ANNA'S GREEK CUISINE
7370 Sawmill Road
Columbus, OH 43235
(614) 799-2207
annasgreekcuisine.com

This strip mall restaurant offers a huge Sunday brunch featuring a spread of homemade Greek favorites. Fill up on moussaka, feta omelets, hummus, lentil soup, lamb, and calamari, plus desserts like Greek yogurt, baklava, and walnut cake.

CHEF'S HOUSE
5454 Roberts Road
Hilliard, OH 43026
(614) 876-5070

A Hilliard family eatery serving big breakfasts of pork chops and eggs, pancakes, breakfast sliders, plus a few Greek specialties like breakfast pitas. And if you like eggs, check out their "double yolk" version.

COLIN'S COFFEE
3714 Riverside Drive
Columbus, OH 43221
(614) 459-0598

Colin's is a tiny coffee shop where the owner - Colin himself - will encourage you to step inside and strike up a conversation. Serving all the standard coffee drinks, plus local bagels, scones, donuts, and breakfast sandwiches, too.

EASY STREET CAFE
5 South Liberty Street
Powell, OH 43065
(614) 888-3279
theeasystreetcafe.com

The Powell Easy Street is the second location of the German Village favorite. Enjoy the colorful bar atmosphere, walls hung with memorabilia, and fun neon lights. Treat yourself to traditional fare, breakfast tacos, fun omelets, or weekend brunch specialties.

FIRST WATCH
3155 Kingsdale Center
Columbus, OH 43221
(614) 538-9866
firstwatch.com
@firstwatch

6768 Perimeter Loop Road
Dublin, OH 43017
(614) 799-2774

3800 Fishinger Boulevard
Columbus, OH 43026
(614) 876-4957
Northwest Columbus has three locations of the small chain, in Dublin, on Fishinger Road, and in the Kingsdale Shopping Center in Upper Arlington. Comfortable pastel decor and a touch of the Florida Keys complement breakfasts of multigrain pancakes, stuffed crepes, and Mexican-themed specialties.

GRAND DAY CAFÉ
1284 West Fifth Avenue
Columbus, OH 43212
(614) 481-3363
granddaycafe.com
@granddaycafe
Grand Day is a little Grandview casual cafe with a big menu of breakfast classics in addition to some one-of-a-kind finds. Try their full range of benedicts, from florentine to blackstone to fried chicken. Or pick up a breakfast quesadilla or an omelet loaded with just about everything. Grand Day is also the only place in town you can get a version of a Kentucky Hot Brown for breakfast: turkey, poached eggs, and bacon on Texas toast with hollandaise.

GREEK TO ME
4697 Reed Road
Columbus, OH 43220
(614) 725-4323
Greek To Me is a little family-run shop at the corner space of a Henderson Road shopping center. Breakfast focuses on omelets, with potato, gyro, Greek, and veggie versions. You can also pick up pancakes, French toast, or breakfast bagel sandwiches.

HELLAS CARRYOUT
9346 Dublin Road
Powell, OH 43065
(614) 792-5494
Hellas is a bustling little diner; its tables, counter space, and even picnic tables out front are crowded with regulars. Omelets are the specialty here. Work your way through two menu pages listing Mexican ones, meat and veggie options, and even premium versions featuring Greek, Italian, and seafood ingredients. Hellas' proximity to the Columbus Zoo makes it a good start to a day trip!

THE HILLS MARKET
7860 Olentangy River Road
Columbus, OH 43235
(614) 846-3220
thehillsmarket.com
@hillsmarket
One of Columbus' few remaining local grocery stores and markets, The Hills can be found on Route 315, just north of the 270 loop. In addition to all of your grocery shopping needs, Hills also serves breakfast on the weekends out on their patio in the warmer months. Show up for one of their pancake breakfasts, or take advantage of Leslie's Creperie food cart, which has set up shop selling their sweet and savory breakfast crepes.

HONEY DIP DONUTS & DINER

4480 Kenny Road
Columbus, OH 43220
(614) 459-0812

A Kenny Road classic, Honey Dip is your quintessential small donut shop. Old school counter and stools. Decent coffee. Pink shelves packed with all things donut: old fashioned cake, specialty honey dip, Bavarian cream, chocolate frosted, devil's food, and everything in between. Recent renovations have added "Diner" to the name, so customers can now enjoy omelets, pancakes, home fries, and eggs along with their baked goods.

JAVA JAN GOURMET COFFEE

16 North High Street
Dublin, OH 43017
(614) 792-5282
javajangourmetcoffee.com
@javajancoffee

A cozy little coffee shop nestled in the heart of downtown Dublin. Java Jan serves up all of your favorite coffee drinks: espresso, lattes, tea, iced coffee, frappes, and smoothies.

KITAMU COFFEE

3221 Hilliard Rome Road
Hilliard, OH 43026
(614) 282-4824
@kitamucoffee

This Hilliard coffee joint serves Stauf's coffee, smoothies, and baked goods made in the neighborhood. Stay late for live music and open mic nights.

LA CHATELAINE

1550 West Lane Avenue
Columbus, OH 43221
(614) 488-1911
lachatelainebakery.com

65 West Bridge Street
Dublin, OH 43017
(614) 763-7151

These are two more locations of Columbus' French bakery and cafe chain. Try delectable omelets or quiches, or order a Petit Déjeuner Français, which pairs coffee with one of their amazingly photogenic pastries.

LEE GARDEN

2685 Federated Boulevard
Columbus, OH 43235
(614) 764-1525

Lee Garden features as one of Columbus' top dim sum stops. Full dim sum is served on weekends. Go with a small group, enjoy some tea, and select small dishes from the carts that are rolled up tableside. Choose from fried and steamed dumplings, stuffed lotus leaves, or more adventurous fare like chicken feet and tripe.

LIL DONUT FACTORY

4543 Scioto Darby Road
Hilliard, OH 43228
(614) 876-9869

This lil Hilliard donut shop sports the goods with cake and glazed donuts, jelly- or cream-filled, longjohns, and rolls. A cheap snack easily paired with coffee, milk, or some orange juice!

A TRIP TO DER DUTCHMAN

445 South Jefferson Avenue, Plain City, OH 43064 | (614) 873-3414 | derdutchman.com

If you want to get a big reaction out of a Columbus resident, try uttering the phrase "Der Dutchman donuts" and see what happens. Our city is home to many great donut joints, but Der Dutchman's in particular will set people salivating and chattering. There are four Der Dutchman's scattered across the central belt of Ohio; Columbus' closet stop is about 30 minutes northwest of us in Plain City.

The massive restaurant is built to handle literal busloads of customers who flock to this model Amish or Dutch (read: Pennsylvania Dutch) country-cooking family restaurant. These spots offer huge meals of comfort food: Amish scrambles, cornmeal mush, hotcakes, omelets, bacon, toast, oatmeal, and on and on. In fact, if you're having trouble choosing a single dish, you can visit their all-you-can-eat breakfast buffet. It's a steal at under $8.00, and features everything you could ask for in a morning meal, including their donuts. It's a breakfast writer's dream. You can show up with the entire extended family, too: there's a giant waiting area, bakery, and gift shop, and dining room after dining room that can accommodate large groups. Even if you're full from the buffet, you still need to take home a box of their longjohns. And if the drive to Plain City is too much for you, take heart: their website conveniently lists where you can pick up their donuts in and around Columbus.

LOUIE'S GRILL FUSION RESTAURANT

4453 Cemetery Road
Hilliard, OH 43026
(614) 777-5606
louiesgrillfusionrestaurant.com

3051 Northwest Boulevard
Columbus, OH 43221
(614) 670-8582

Louie's has two locations: the original on Cemetery Road in Hilliard, and a newer one in Upper Arlington's Kingsdale shopping center. Both restaurants sport a fusion of Mexican, Italian, and American food, although much of breakfast focuses on the Mexican and American side of things. Try some classic pancakes or French toast, or some huevos rancheros, enchiladas, or machaca, which includes beef brisket, black beans, veggies, chips, and ranchero sauce.

LUCK BROS' COFFEE HOUSE

1101 West First Avenue
Columbus, OH 43212
(614) 299-9330
luckbroscoffeehouse.com
@luckbros

If you want to learn about coffee in Columbus, sit and learn at the feet of Andy Luck. His coffee shop serves pastries and a homemade breakfast bake (using Andy's family's recipe), but the full experience there includes a stop at the brew bar. Watch as Andy and his crew prepare single cups of his hand-selected roasts to exact specifications using the best equipment. A great way to learn how coffee should really be brewed and tasted!

MARSHALL'S RESTAURANT

1105 West First Avenue
Columbus, OH 43212
(614) 294-1105
marshallsonline.com

Marshall's has been a Grandview favorite for over 25 years. Regulars visit for crabcake omelets, breakfast sandwiches, and sausage gravy and biscuits. Early risers can sneak in for cheap Tuesday through Saturday specials.

SIDE DISH:
BAGEL DELIVERY

If you're not willing to travel for your New York bagels, they can come to you! *Sammy's Bagels* delivers fresh bagels, muffins, pastries, challah, and more straight to your door. Choose from over twenty types of bagels, plus all the cream cheese fixings. Place an order online (www.sammysbagels.net) or call (614) 252-1551 to bring Sammy's home to you.

NEIGHBOR'S DELI

2142 West Henderson Road
Columbus, OH 43220
(614) 459-0188

A small hole-in-the-wall deli, serving breakfast sandwiches deli-style. Try one with fried egg and pastrami, or one with cheese steak and eggs. Also serving bagels, plus juice and coffee.

THE OLIVE TREE MEDITERRANEAN CAFE

3185 Hilliard-Rome Road
Hilliard, OH 43026
(614) 527-8812
olivetreecolumbus.net
@olivetreecafe

Head out to Olive Tree for a unique Mediterranean breakfast spread on Sundays. You can try dishes like shakshuka, an Israeli and North African dish of eggs poached with spicy veggies; you can add Moroccan Merguez sausage to it, too. Or dine on jachnun, a Jewish dish of rolled pastry baked in layers and served with eggs, tomato, and a hot pepper puree.

PAUL'S FIFTH AVENUE
1565 West Fifth Avenue
Columbus, OH 43212
(614) 481-8848
paulsonline.com
Paul's, or Paul's Pantry as it's still called by some, is a Grandview institution. Regulars have gathered for decades for pancakes, sandwiches, and eggs cooked however you like. But the real reason the crowds eat at Paul's are the callahans: omelet ingredients served over a giant bed of home fries.

SCRAMBLER MARIE'S
3980 Presidential Parkway
Powell, OH 43065
(614) 760-7220
scramblermaries.com
@scramblermaries

5291 Nike Station
Hilliard, OH 43026
(614) 850-7243
There are two Scrambler's locations in this corner of Columbus' breakfast scene. Scrambler's is a Toledo-based chain with a solid presence around town. Customers love their big breakfast menu. Items on the menu are named after Marie's family. Try smaller portions of Emily's Right Bites or go the other direction with the heart-stopping Uncle Moose's Manhandler.

SPIRO'S PLAZA CAFE AT THE QUARRY
2958 McKinley Avenue
Columbus, OH 43204
(614) 481-8448
spiroscafe.com
The quarry location is the latest spot for a cafe that's been in business since 1971. Run by husband and wife Vicki and Dimitrios Papadimitriou, the cafe has settled across from the series of small lakes and quarries in western Columbus. Come here for classics like Greek omelets, pork chops and eggs, or their popular breakfast sandwich.

SUNNY STREET CAFÉ
7573 Sawmill Road
Dublin, OH 43016
(614) 932-7008
sunnystreetcafe.com
@sunnystreetcafe

7042 Hospital Drive
Dublin, OH 43017
(614) 389-3640
There are two Sunny Street locations in Dublin, each one located near a Kroger shopping center. The cafes offer a bright and casual atmosphere while you feast on chicken fried steak, Denver omelets, or eggs benedicts topped with spinach, feta, and tomatoes.

SWEET CLOVE SUNSHINE CAFE
6630 Sawmill Road
Dublin, OH 43235
(614) 764-1717
sweetclove.com
Columbus has long been known as a test market, and Sweet Clove demonstrates that yet again. The Honey Baked Ham company, known for their sweet glazed, spiral-cut hams, opened what is to be the first of many cafes in the fall of 2010. This concept store features a brightly painted country kitchen decor. Signature dishes include heaping piles of eggs benedict, French toast (with massive dollops of homemade whipped cream), and omelets. Many of the dishes feature their well-known ham.

THE ORIGINAL GOODIE SHOP
2116 Tremont Center
Columbus, OH 43221
(614) 488-8777
theoriginalgoodieshop.com
@goodieshop
In the Tremont Center, just doors down from Chef-O-Nette diner (see feature), is another Upper Arlington institution: the Goodie Shop. This family bakery has been serving the good stuff for over five decades. Line up for cake donuts, cinnamon sticks, bismarcks, coffee cake, danishes, muffins... oh, who are we kidding? Just get all of it.

NORTHEAST

BEECHWOLD, WORTHINGTON, WESTERVILLE, EASTON, POLARIS

Our northeast corner includes a broad range of neighborhoods and thus a healthy mix of breakfast options. Morse Road and Route 161, for instance, have become known for a variety of ethnic eateries. This area also includes Beechwold, the expanse between Clintonville and Worthington, as well as two of Columbus' major shopping centers: Easton Town Center and Polaris Fashion Place. But it's not all big and corporate up here; Worthington and Westerville have their own little downtowns, which are packed with great donut shops, brunches, coffee shops, and pubs.

AFRICAN PARADISE

2263 Morse Road
Columbus, OH 43229

(614) 476-2163

africanparadise.itgo.com

Columbus is home to a very large Somali population, one of the largest in the world outside of Somalia itself, and out of that a number of Somali restaurants have been established. African served boneless when it comes to breakfast. Both suqaar dishes can be served with "bread," which is called *jibati* (or chapati), a grilled flatbread. Another option is *angro* (pronounced an-JER-o; sometimes

"Somalis typically don't eat a dry meal in the morning, so breakfast dishes, while similar in make-up to lunch or dinner fare, are served in a light gravy."

Paradise is situated on Morse Road, an area of town becoming known for its high quality ethnic eateries. The restaurant itself is set back from the road, in a small strip of buildings that stand behind a few other restaurants. You'll find the restaurant in a strip with a Somali market and Muslim community center; most mornings you can expect to see the group of older men relaxing out front with their coffee.

The interior is dimly lit, but still very welcoming for guests. African Paradise has been in business over thirteen years, and Adam Mohamed, who has been a manager for three years, thrives on sharing Somali food and customs with his guests. There are a few different dining areas in the restaurant with separate rooms for groups of just men or just women, as well as areas for families. The back room includes the seating area exclusively for women, as well as prayer room.

A Somali breakfast - *quraac* - typically begins with juice, tea, and fruit. African Paradise serves a range of juices, including mango, pineapple, and watermelon. The tea (called *shaah*) is an incredibly flavorful blend that includes cinnamon sticks, sugar, black pepper, and many more spices.

Somalis typically don't eat a dry meal in the morning, so breakfast dishes, while similar in make-up to lunch or dinner fare, are served in a light gravy. Two of the features are chicken or beef suqaar. *Suqaar* means grilled, so the meat is grilled and served with a mix of onions, tomatoes, bell peppers, garlic, and spices. Beef suqaar is cooked with carrots and potatoes as well. Generally, meat is

spelled canjeero), which is a moist, spongy bread similar to Ethiopian injera. A diner will tear pieces of the bread and use those to scoop up bites of food.

Other breakfast favorites include beef or lamb liver chunks stewed in vegetables and spices or *foul* (sometimes spelled *ful*), a dish comprised of fava beans, tomatoes, and onions, eaten with jibati. Or, you can try an African omelet, a sweeter dish made with flour, sugar, and eggs.

LA CHATELAINE

627 North High Street
Worthington, OH 43085

(614) 848-6711

lachatelainebakery.com

"Bonjour!" That's how you're greeted any time you call or step into La Chatelaine. You might not expect to find a French country kitchen in the middle of Ohio, but La Chatelaine can certainly make you feel like you're sitting in one. The dining room surrounds you with wood, brick, and stone. Wooden beams cross the ceiling. Edith Piaf songs play quietly. There are little cafe tables if it's just the two of you, or you can seat the entire family at one of the giant wooden dining tables.

"Breakfast at La Chatelaine can be light or filling, but whatever you choose, it will be beautiful."

Owners Stan and Gigi Wielezynski created such an atmosphere by importing a little bit of their home. Inspired by Stan's family's country estate in Normandy, France, they sought to bring the hospitality of early French restaurants to Ohio. The restaurant originated with their location on Lane Avenue, where you can still find them working, and has now expanded to three total. Each of their children is involved, too. You'll find them around town, cooking, managing the different locations, and welcoming customers.

Breakfast at La Chatelaine can be light or filling, but whatever you choose, it will be beautiful. Try some hot chocolate, a cappuccino, or some Harney & Sons tea. Enjoy a simple meal of the Petit Déjeuner Français (literally, a "small French breakfast"), which pairs one of their exquisite pastries with a cup of Stauf's coffee. Choose from croissants, beignets, pinwheels, macaroons, muffins, cookies, and more. Half the fun is simply gazing at the shelves of baked goods, or watching them come straight out of the brick oven.

You can make your way down the cafeteria line and order something more substantial, too. Choose from Parisienne or Provençal omelets, with a mix of meats, cheeses, vegetables, and herbs. The quiches come filled with bacon, mushrooms, or chicken and spinach. Specialty omelets and quiches rotate through the menu as well. But perhaps the most picturesque of their breakfast offerings are the cocottes: miniature casseroles of eggs, meat, cheese, and vegetables baked and served in small iron pots, often adorned with beautifully carved vegetables.

The Worthington location of La Chatelaine benefits from a giant brick patio along North High Street. It's an excellent place to start a day of wandering Olde Worthington, or a welcome respite on Saturdays when the Farmer's Market is in season.

LINDEN CAFE

1393 Cleveland Avenue
Columbus, OH 43211

(614) 754-1054

lindencafecolumbus.com

The Linden Café brought chicken and waffles to Columbus. The dish is a soul food classic, sure, but it was Keith Griffea, the original owner of the Café, who first introduced the dish to our fair city.

The Café itself came into being in 2000, as part of Mayor Coleman's Urban Growth program. In rejuvenating the South Linden neighborhood, the program rebuilt the corner of Cleveland and 11th Avenues, and offered assistance to entrepreneurs looking to get their start. They asked Chef Keith to start a coffee shop on the corner, but he knew better. When he sat in the empty space, he knew he wanted something that would connect in a more meaningful way to the neighborhood. He envisioned a cafe serving soul food classics, with chicken and waffles at the forefront. The result was a Linden, and a Columbus, mainstay.

"Keith says, "It looks like something served at Easton, but tastes like something grandma made.""

But it's not just all chicken this and waffles that at the Linden Café. Michael Mayfield, the current owner, puts together a simple breakfast menu of omelets, breakfast sandwiches, and pancakes, plus comfort food mainstays like grits, hash browns, turkey sausage, and Texas toast.

The chicken and waffles are still the focus. You can order chicken wings or strips; either way, the chicken is moist and tender. Chef Mike brines the chicken overnight, seasons it, and fries it to perfection. His special waffle batter includes hints of nutmeg and vanilla, giving you some warm and cakey waffles: the perfect landing pad for a pile of fried chicken. Garnishes create a presentation that, as Keith says, "looks like something served at Easton, but tastes like something grandma made."

The cafe itself is comfortable, with a big counter decorated with stone, cool colors, and big windows looking out on the neighborhood. Soft jazz adds a relaxing touch.

While they're upholding the proud tradition of chicken and waffles, Chef Mike and his crew are still experimenting with the form. Newer variations include a southwestern style with corn, black beans, and salsa, flavored with a chili-spiked honey. There are also country scallion and bacon, macaroni and cheese versions, and possibly even a portable version, served in a waffle cone.

NORTHSTAR CAFE

4015 Townsfair Way
Columbus, OH 43219

(614) 532-5444

thenorthstarcafe.com

If you do a Google search for "Columbus breakfast," you're bound to find at least one of the Northstar locations in the list. The first Northstar Café opened in 2004 in the Short North and quickly became a signature stop on any Columbus breakfast tour. There are now three locations: the Beechwold edition opened in 2007, while Easton joined up in 2010. It started as a partnership between Kevin and Katy Malhame, and Kevin's brother Darren. Kevin and Katy had worked a long time as restaurant managers, liking the experience but always wanting to open their own eatery dedicated to a positive environmental and community impact. In short, they hoped to create a dining experience focused on "pure ingredients prepared in unadulterated ways," Kevin says.

Each location is slightly different in size and shape, which creates a different flow and feel to the restaurants. At every one, however, customers line up to order at the counter, take a number, then find a table. (Quick note: be nice to your fellow breakfasters and obey the signs: don't claim a table until you've ordered and have a number.) Employees will deliver the food to your table; drinks are all self service.

Easton, the latest to join the Northstar ranks, offers two levels of dining, plus a patio. The interior of each Northstar - but Easton especially - is magnificent and detailed. The thoughtful design integrates the shape of each location, and focuses on wooden construction and natural light. Just

order, and watch the bakers and chefs hard at work through the big glass windows.

Many of Northstar's breakfast dishes have become local legends in their own right. The Cloud Nine Pancakes, made with a light ricotta cheese in the batter, are fluffy and golden, topped with bananas

and maple syrup. The Big Burrito is a giant grilled burrito stuffed with sweet potatoes, red peppers, grilled onions, black beans, a fried egg, and white cheddar (this is one of the author's favorite breakfast dishes; hint: add bacon to it). Other dishes include a turkey and sweet potato hash and a mushroom frittata; you can easily smell either one of these as a

"Many of Northstar's breakfast dishes have become local legends in their own right."

like their food, Kevin says, they designed the restaurant itself to be simple and real. As they were building the Easton location, he says, their landlord wandered in and marveled at the place. When he asked how they got the tables to look like mahogany and ash, Kevin pointed out that they simply used mahogany and ash. You also get an open view of the kitchens at each location. At Easton, you can look to your right while waiting to

server carries them through the restaurant. Dishes vary by location; the Easton branch also specializes in Proscuitto and Poached Eggs, served on a toasted focaccia bread with parmesan cheese. The breakfast menu is complemented by a range of coffees, plus fresh-squeezed orange juice or smoothies made with fresh fruits and vegetables. On top of all this, they serve a range of baked goods like their Morning Glory Muffin and Ham and Cheese Scones.

THE BEST BREAKFAST & SANDWICHES

5916 Westerville Road
Westerville, OH 43081

(614) 776-5788

thebestrestaurant.info

@thebestbfast

Tom and Jan Spangler have worked in restaurants much of their lives. They both originally hail from Ohio, but took a long path around the country before returning to Columbus and eventually opening their own place. Tom has been in the business since ninth grade, when he took his first job as a dishwasher in an Italian restaurant, mainly because his high school

> ## "The Best exudes that *Cheers*-like sensibility that all true mom-and-pop neighborhood diners have."

teachers wanted to keep him busy and out of trouble. In college he worked as a bartender, and worked his way up to being a General Manager of a T.G.I. Friday's by the time he was 21. Tom spent the following years as a "fixer" for chain restaurants, traveling from Denver to Dallas to Charlotte and all over to help chain locations keep up with corporate standards. He and Jan met while working at an Applebee's; he knew the management side of restaurants, she knew the service and hospitality. They worked together for a while as acquaintances, then parted ways for thirteen years. After that time, they found each other again, settled in Columbus, and got married. Hitting a lull in their careers working for corporate chains, they decided it was time to be their own bosses.

So it was that Tom and Jan created their own restaurant, and named it by the standards they keep: The Best Breakfast and Sandwiches. Their goal, says Tom, was to create the "least corporate" restaurant possible: one that was unique, with a loyal staff that knew their customers, and that served honest, made-in-front-of-you comfort food for breakfast and lunch.

The concept started with the bread, and customers love The Best for it still. Thick slices of white, whole grain, and rye bread complement nearly every meal.

It's perfect for stacking with scrambled eggs, makes for great French toast, and rounds out the best reuben. Tom initially purchased the bread from a friend of his in Lewis Center, Ohio; when the friend went out of business, Tom bought the recipes and still has them baked specially for his restaurant.

The Best exudes that *Cheers*-like sensibility that all true mom-and-pop neighborhood diners have. Visit once, and Tom, Jan, Suzanne, Kelly, Brian, Karen, Tonya, Dennis, Chris, Harry - the whole gang - will get to know you. So the next time you walk in the door, they'll know your name and ask about your work, your family, your recent vacation, everything.

Cooks at The Best know their customers so well that, Tom says, tickets will come up with just their names on it, like "John's omelet" or "Ted's corned beef hash." These are little customized orders named after regulars, and often known only to one or two of the cooks. Some have even made their way onto the menu. The RonRob Healthy Choice is named after two customers - Ron and Rob, obviously - who ordered the same healthy dish of sauteed ham and veggies over toast, with over easy eggs.

Other Best classics include their corned beef hash, specially made with meat from a local producer and sliced fresh at the restaurant, or the big stacks of pancakes, giant omelets, or the hard-to-find SOS (creamed chipped beef on toast). But no matter what you order, regulars will insist, of course, that it's the best.

EXTRA HELPINGS

BILAN CAFE RESTAURANT
3949 Cleveland Avenue
Columbus, OH 43224
(614) 337-2442
A Somali eatery doing breakfast most mornings of the week. Expect a fairly laid back atmosphere, and be ready to roll with a changing menu. Somali breakfast typically begins with tea and juice, includes fruit, and features dishes like chicken or beef grilled with vegetables and served in a light gravy. Most meals are served with a grilled flatbread called chapati (or jibati) that customers use to scoop up bites of food.

DAYBREAK DINER
1168 East Weber Road
Columbus, OH 43211
(614) 261-4560
daybreakdiner.net
@daybreakdiner
A newer spot in Linden, Daybreak is the dream of owner Bill Kinniard, who always wanted to own his own diner. He produces all the diner favorites, including some killer hash browns, plus fun extras like Captain Crunch French toast, breakfast fried rice, and cheeseburger omelets.

FIRST WATCH
116 Worthington Mall
Worthington, OH 43085
(614) 431-9040
firstwatch.com
@firstwatch

4770 Morse Road
Columbus, OH 43230
(614) 475-8512

2103 Polaris Parkway
Columbus, OH 43240
(614) 846-2738
Often voted one of the top breakfasts in Columbus, this chain boasts multiple locations around town. In our northeast corner you'll find three: one off High Street in Worthington; one on Morse Road, east of the 270 loop; and one in the eastern portions of Polaris Parkway. All three restaurants serve lighter (but still filling) breakfast fare like multigrain pancakes, turkey sausage gravy, or egg crepes with turkey and avocado.

FITZY'S OLD FASHIONED DINER
1487 Schrock Road
Columbus, OH 43229
(614) 846-1004
eatatfitzys.com
As one of Columbus' few twenty-four hour diners, Fitzy's is the place for every crowd. You can join the third shift workers, the late night college students, or the quieter folks in the morning. Owner Mike Lott loves creating a welcoming spot for his regulars. He serves up huge plates of comfort food: potatoes, steak and eggs, bologna, pancakes, and more.

GENA'S RESTAURANT

5947 South Sunbury Road
Westerville, OH 43081
(614) 895-0089

This one-room Westerville eatery makes a name for itself by boasting "The Greatest American Pecan Roll," a giant nutty roll sliced in half and grilled. If you're a fan of *Man v. Food*-style eating, you can tackle their three-pancake challenge. Only about 25 people have eaten the gigantic stack over seven years.

GEORGE'S BEECHWOLD DINER

4408 Indianola Avenue
Columbus, OH 43214
(614) 447-0944

The Beechwold Diner opened in early 2010 in the space formerly occupied by Rube's Diner. Rube's was a greasy hole-in-a-wall if there ever was one, and the new owners cleaned and renovated the space to give it new life. Owners were concerned whether Beechwold could handle a new diner; the first hour they opened, no one showed up. But then the customers poured in. If you were a fan of Rube's, take heart: one of the cooks from Rube's now mans the grill.

HEAVENLY CUP ESPRESSO

25 North State Street
Westerville, OH 43081
(614) 523-3306
heavenlycupespresso.com
@heavenlycup1

Heavenly Cup is a cozy coffee shop nestled in uptown Westerville, serving coffee, pastries, and basic breakfast favorites like quiche. The small space doesn't allow a lot of seating, but tables out front give you a chance to relax while strolling and shopping around the neighborhood.

JAVA CENTRAL CAFE & GIFTS

20 South State Street
Westerville, OH 43081
(614) 839-0698
java-central.com

Another coffee shop in uptown Westerville. Java Central roasts their own beans and creates a huge menu of different coffee drinks, hot chocolate, and chai. Enjoy the art gallery, gift shop, or some local music while you visit, or order some whole beans to take home and brew yourself!

MIMI'S CAFE

1428 Polaris Parkway
Columbus, OH 43240
(614) 433-0441
mimiscafe.com
@mimis_cafe

The single Columbus edition of a slightly upscale cafe chain owned by Bob Evans Restaurants, located along shopping-centric Polaris Parkway just north of Columbus. Featuring a menu of omelets, breakfast wraps, pancakes, or the faux French-themed menu of croissants, benedicts, and quiches.

MUDSLINGER'S DRIVE-THRU COFFEE

5755 Maxtown Road
Westerville, OH 43082
(614) 895-6833
mudslingersdrivethrucoffee.com
@mudslingers1

Westerville loves its coffee! If you're on the go, try this little coffee kiosk, serving a host of coffee drinks, tea, smoothies, and fresh made mini donuts. You can also order up their coffee beans to take with you.

BREAKFAST AT FARMERS MARKETS

From spring until late fall, Columbus' farmers markets are filled with residents seeking fresh fruits and vegetables, delicious meats, and homemade pastries, pies, and cookies. Wherever you prefer to do your farmers market shopping, it's worth finding yourself a simple breakfast to keep yourself fed and happy. You can snack on buckets of blueberries, sip a cup of fresh coffee, or munch the loads of fresh baked goods while you stroll the market.

At the Worthington Farmers Market, for instance, you'll find the absolutely picturesque baked goods of *Sassafras Bakery*, served by the lovely A.J. Perry. You can't go wrong when starting your market trip with a rotating menu that has included potato bacon pocket pies, cinnamon rolls, coffee cake muffins, kitchen sink granola bars, and caramelized onion brie scones. Stop by early: not surprisingly, A.J.'s creations sell out quickly!

Further south at the Clintonville Farmers Market, Daniel Riesenberger of *Dan the Baker* makes and quickly sells artisan breads like sourdough croissants and savory baguettes. Daniel's work is indicative of the best that farmers markets have to offer: a small business owner with passion, creating a product that people love.

Worthington and Clintonville are just two of the many markets around town. Market seasons, hours, vendors, and locations vary, so it's worth checking their websites as you seek out farmers market breakfasts:

Bexley: bexleyfarmersmarket.com
Blendon Township: blendontwp.org
Clintonville: clintonvillefarmersmarket.org
Columbus Commons: columbuscommons.org
Dublin: dublinfarmersmarket.com
Easton: eastonfarmersmarket.com
Grandview: fifthbynorthwest.org
Grove City: gcchamber.org
Market at 15th & High: wexarts.org
New Albany: nafarmersmarket.com
North Market: northmarket.com
Olde Worthington: owba.net
Pearl Market: downtowncolumbus.com/pearlmarket
Powell: visitpowell.com

NORTHSTAR CAFÉ

4241 North High Street
Columbus, OH 43214
(614) 784-2233
thenorthstarcafe.com

This is the second location of the popular Northstar Cafe trio. The space here is long and thin, with rows of communal benches and small booths, plus a bright patio overlooking High Street. Try favorite dishes like ricotta pancakes, breakfast burritos, or turkey hash, and top them off with fresh orange juice, coffee, and fruit smoothies.

P.K. O'RYANS IRISH PUB & RESTAURANT

666 High Street
Worthington, OH 43085
(614) 781-0770
pkoryans.com

In downtown Olde Worthington, you can grab breakfast at this little Irish pub every day of the week. Start an average Monday or a busy farmer's market Saturday either in the restaurant or out on the front patio with breakfast standards like pancakes, omelets, or a simple breakfast of eggs, bacon, and hash browns.

THE PANCAKE HOUSE

129 West Schrock Road
Westerville, OH 43081
(614) 898-6500

A newer addition to the cheap little diner scene in Columbus. Located in Westerville, the Pancake House features all of the diner favorites in a one-room restaurant. Foremost on the menu are, of course, the pancakes with buttermilk, buckwheat, and cornmeal varieties. These are topped with anything from apples, blueberries, and peaches to pecans and chocolate chips. You can even order pancake sandwiches!

POMEGRANATE MEDITERRANEAN CUISINE

5239 North Hamilton Road
Columbus, OH 43230
(614) 478-1595
pommedcuisine.com

This restaurant does a weekend breakfast of classic dishes like eggs, pancakes, and Monte Cristo sandwiches, but also features skillets, burritos, omelets, and more, many of which have a Mediterranean flair. The Mediterranean Breakfast Burrito, for instance, comes with eggs, red peppers, onions, spinach, feta, and gyro meat. Or the Mediterranean Breakfast Skillet combines home fries, eggs, veggies, and gyro meat, and tops them with a homemade gyro gravy.

SCHNEIDER'S BAKERY

6 South State Street
Westerville, OH 43081
(614) 882-6611

Schneider's donuts have been popular since the late 1950's, and if you really want to experience them fresh, you'll need to live like a college student. College kids, especially from nearby Otterbein University, regularly gather in uptown Westerville to catch fresh donuts when the bakery opens... at about 1 a.m. Rain or snow, summer or winter. Join the crowd for a box of favorites, or opt for muffins, rolls, croissants, and other breads.

SCRAMBLER MARIE'S

6152 Cleveland Avenue
Columbus, OH 43231
(614) 901-9604
scramblermaries.com
@scramblermaries

8679 Sancus Boulevard
Columbus, OH 43240
(614) 846-7786

5729 North Hamilton Road
Columbus, OH 43230
(614) 337-1020

The northeast corner of Columbus enjoys three locations of this Toledo-based chain. The first can be found off busy Cleveland Avenue in a strip mall; the second stands alone off even busier Polaris Parkway; the third is located outside the 270 loop on Hamilton Road. Regulars gather in these green and yellow restaurants serving consistent breakfast dishes named after Marie's family members, like Andrew's All Americans, Peter's Brunch Wraps, or Melanie Marie's Skillets.

SHADES RESTAURANT

983 East Fifth Avenue
Columbus, Oh 43201
(614) 291-6555

Located on Fifth Avenue in the Milo-Grogan neighborhood, Shades is the breakfast version of the dive bar. It was originally associated with the Shades on the South Side, but was sold off by the Shades family and only retains the name now. Enjoy eggs, pancakes, all the breakfast standards while watching the cook at the grill.

SUNNY STREET CAFÉ

644 North State Street
Westerville, OH 43082
(614) 899-6113
sunnystreetcafe.com

The Westerville location of a small chain of brightly colored casual cafes found in Ohio, Missouri, and Texas. Often attached to shopping centers, these cafes feature a very likeable breakfast menu full of customizable omelets, benedicts, a range of pancakes, even loaded hash browns and stuffed biscuits and gravy.

TEE JAYE'S COUNTRY PLACE

4910 North High Street
Columbus, OH 43214
(614) 885-1383
barnyardbuster.com
@teejayes

Recognizable by the big neon arrow sign at the corner of Morse and High Streets, this location of the central Ohio chain is open twenty-four hours a day, serving cornmeal pancakes, sausage cornbread, and their famous Barnyard Buster, a platter of biscuits, eggs, and potatoes smothered in sausage gravy. How popular is the BB? It's TeeJaye's website: barnyardbuster.com.

WESTERVILLE GRILL

59 South State Street
Westerville, Oh 43081
(614) 794-7200

At the southern end of uptown Westerville is a one-room eatery serving breakfast all day, every day. Begin your day with fresh made corned beef hash, monster omelets, and eggs benedict or florentine, made with grilled tomato, spinach, and cheese.

CENTRAL

DOWNTOWN, SHORT NORTH, CAMPUS, OLD NORTH, CLINTONVILLE

The central section of our Columbus breakfast map is rife with fine breakfast fare. A growing downtown, sparkling arts district, active university, and lively Old North/Clintonville neighborhoods means that you can find any type of breakfast at all hours of the day. Look for everything here from old-school diners, student-favorite donut shops, late-night hangouts, and business-favorite sandwich joints! As this section includes some of the oldest parts of Columbus, you'll find a lot of delicious eats that are steeped in tradition.

BUCKEYE DONUTS

1998 North High Street
Columbus, OH 43210

(614) 391-3923

buckeye-donuts.com

In the 1960's, a big wave of Greek immigrants reached the United States, and many of them started small restaurants serving donuts. Enter the Barouxis family, who opened a donut joint called Jolly Roger in 1969. Grandfather Jimmy and father George learned donut making on the spot, having never done it before. They lucked out in finding a location right across the street from one of the country's largest universities: The Ohio State University. There they began a tradition of serving fresh donuts twenty-four hours a day to hungry college students. The only major change came in 1979, when they renamed the restaurant to Buckeye Donuts. Now at the helm is the third generation, led by Jimmy Barouxis along with his mother Toula. Jimmy went to school at Ohio State and earned a business degree, but knew all along that he would take over the family business someday, which he did in 2001.

"It's easy to see why returning alumni relive their late nights as university students nostalgically with some buttermilk donuts or Bismarcks."

Jimmy and his crew make roughly 2000 donuts throughout the day. All of their recipes exist in their memories. One of the primary donut makers is Yanni Agalos, who you'll find in the back swiftly rolling out cinnamon rolls and drizzling donut glaze, like he's been doing for thirty-five years. He and Jimmy converse exclusively in Greek; when Yanni came to the United States in 1977, the Barouxis family hired him immediately. It's the only job he's ever had in Columbus.

Donuts are an easy and inexpensive snack for college students, and when they're made like those at Buckeye Donuts, it's easy to see why

returning alumni relive their late nights as university students nostalgically with some buttermilk donuts or Bismarcks. While the donuts are a big seller, Buckeye Donuts' breakfast sandwiches make up

nearly half their business. The sandwiches are a simple to-go food for students: choose bacon, ham, or sausage with egg and cheese on a bagel, croissant, or Texas toast.

Walking through the front door puts you face-to-face with trays jammed full of goodies. You can begin with a cakey buttermilk donut: try a strawberry, blueberry, or pumpkin-flavored one. Work your way through the cream- or custard-filled, the sprinkled, the sugar-dusted, or the chocolate-coated. When you're through with those, turn your attention to the "fancy" donuts in the lower cases: chunky apple fritters, chocolate-covered Buckeye donuts dabbed with peanut butter, or longjohns filled with cream.

Buckeye Donuts crosses the decor of an old diner with that of an Ohio State student's dorm room. A small curved counter lets you sit and study. Scarlet and gray tiles decorate the floor. Bits of pop culture pepper the walls: Star Wars, the Beatles, Curious George, alongside plenty of Ohio State memorabilia. Intertwined with these are pictures of Buckeye Donut history, showing the Barouxis family hard at work.

JACK'S SANDWICH SHOP

52 East Lynn Street
Columbus, OH 43215

(614) 224-3655

jacksdowntowndiner.com

Jack's was once one of three diners in downtown Columbus started by Jack and Ida Holt in 1942. Jack had returned from World War II and decided to open the diners in Columbus' (and Ohio's) financial

Beer bottles, milk shake machines, and a black and yellow sign that boasts, "We Read the Dispatch." The store even uses an old rotary telephone to handle the waves of take-out orders.

"On any given day, you can sidle up to the counter along with the business crowd, politicians, construction workers, attorneys, even the mayor of Columbus or the governor of Ohio."

and political center. The original location stood further north up High Street, closer to where the federal building stands now. The current location for Jack's, hidden down Lynn Street, opened in 1968 as a back alley eatery called The Curly Q. It opened as Jack's in 1976, the same year the Rhodes State Office Tower began operation. On any given day, you can sidle up to the counter along with the business crowd, politicians, construction workers, attorneys, even the mayor of Columbus or the governor of Ohio.

The secret to Jack's longevity is its regular customers. Amongst the dedicated crowds, one small group of men stand above the rest: the Lynn Alley Irregulars. This group of businessmen and attorneys met regularly from 1968 until May 2010. Their names are emblazoned on a plaque above their regular table. Only two members survive. Mr. Miller moved to Florida, but you can still spot Mr. Petro sipping coffee at their table. Mr. Petro said there were only two rules governing the group: 1.) you could talk about anything but work, and 2.) if more than one person was there, you had to talk. No reading the paper in silence. The conversation had to flow.

The physical space of the restaurant withstood the test of time, too. Sit at the counter and admire the original grill and flattop, with its distinct orange lights, fake wood paneling, and silver nobs. The delightfully tacky decorations hearken back to the diner's early days, too: Coca-Cola signs, DAD's Root

The current owners Chris and Kathy Kowalski keep the diner's tradition well. They and their crew know all of their regulars, often starting someone's order

the moment they walk through the door. They serve a lot of breakfast all day long, from breakfast sandwiches, golden pancakes (still made using Jack's original recipe), pressed bacon, and steak and eggs.

KATALINA'S
CAFE CORNER

1105 Pennsylvania Avenue
Columbus, OH 43201

(614) 294-2233

cafecornercolumbus.com

@cafecorner

Stepping into Katalina's Café Corner is like entering a warm, welcoming, and cluttered country kitchen. Old red shelves hold coffee, jars of hot sauce, and syrup. A battered chandelier dangles from the ceiling. Old wooden crates are filled with jars and stacks of local magazines. Housemade iced tea is served in mason jars.

When Kathleen took the helm, she introduced breakfast dishes you couldn't find elsewhere in town. Much of the menu has a decided Latin theme, influenced by the cooks in her kitchen. (The name "Katalina" comes from them addressing her in the Spanish form of "Kathleen.") You'll find items like Mexican French Toast, made with Mexican chocolate.

"Stepping into Katalina's Café Corner is like entering a warm, welcoming, and cluttered country kitchen."

Katalina's is the latest iteration of a small building on the corner of Third and Pennsylvania Avenues, in the heart of Harrison West. Initially an auto shop, over the years the corner location served as an ice house, a candle store, and finally began its life in food as a creperie. In the early 2000's, brothers Pete and John Novak renovated the space into a coffee and sandwich shop called Café Corner. They expanded the kitchen, built the patio, and added an overnight breakfast service called Late Night Eggs. The Novaks opened a second LNE next to Ohio State's campus, renamed it Eggfast, and eventually moved their entire operation there.

In December 2009, Kathleen Day took over Café Corner and added her own special touches to the restaurant. She gathered most of her culinary education serving as a cook for a French Countess, learning about "real cooking" from one of the other chefs, in particular the appreciation of fresh ingredients and local produce. Her daily routine included visits to the local market, butcher, baker, and out to the garden, then building meals made simply and with fresh ingredients. Upon her return to the States, and all throughout grad school, she continued cooking and catering. A business marketing job brought her to Columbus, and when Café Corner became available, she saw the opportunity to put her lifelong skills to work and create a quirky neighborhood eatery. Nowadays, you'll also find Ryan Janiszewski behind the counter. He joined Kathleen in 2010, first making deliveries for the Café, and now helping with business and management.

Or the breakfast tacos are loaded with eggs, chorizo, avocado, cheese, plus salsa and hot sauce. The Latin Pancake Balls are filled with Nutella or strawberry preserves. Past specials have included Huevos Rancheros and a Mexican Eggs Benedict, served on a croissant with prosciutto and a chipotle hollandaise.

Katalina's is also one of a few restaurants in town that serve Hens in a Basket (known by many names, including Eggs in a Nest or Toad in a Hole), which are two eggs cooked in a hole cut out of a slice of bread.

Most importantly, Kathleen created a cafe that connects to the community, utilizes local produce, and provides a unique dining experience all day long. The result is a cafe making complicated food that's easy to love.

KNEAD
URBAN DINER

505 North High Street
Columbus, OH 43215

(614) 228-6323

kneadonhigh.com

@kneadonhigh

Rick and Krista Lopez know the Columbus restaurant scene well. They've owned restaurants in town since 1996, first Crescendo Pastaria in Powell and then Trattoria La Tavola in Dublin, and both Italian in focus. As they were looking to start their next project, they knew they needed a few things. Rick knew he needed to start a sandwich shop, and Krista knew she needed to have a bakery. They also knew they needed to move their lives and their business from the suburbs to central Columbus. The combination of these "needs," mixed with a quick bakery pun, resulted in *Knead* Urban Diner.

Rick comes from a background of cooking, with a strong Italian and Spanish influence from his grandparents. Krista, as she says, married into it. Rick also has a background in music; he worked in restaurants during the day, and then played in a band at night. Musicians are inevitably drawn to cooking, Krista says, because they enjoy the "instant gratification of applause" from seeing others enjoy their food. At Knead you'll have the chance to applaud Rick's kitchen creations, including his charcuterie. Go on the right day, and you'll get to sample his bacon, smoked and cured himself, or any of the other meats he's preparing.

farmers clipped to the different counties. These serve as a faster explanation of where the food came from than lines and lines of text describing each menu item. The Lopezes have been at the cusp of the "locavore" movement in Columbus for some time. From their time running La Tavola and Crescendo, and from Rick's years working in restaurants - including a stint as executive chef at the Westin Hotel - they knew to use Ohio sources

"One of the most noticeable features of Knead is the large magnetized map of Ohio, with all 88 counties marked in different shades of reds, browns, and creams."

Breakfast at Knead is typically served on weekends, and common menu items include sausage gravy poured over homemade biscuits or a frittata loaded with veggies. Don't forget the bakery portion of Knead as well. Krista creates biscuits, muffins, cinnamon rolls, scones, breads, even homemade versions of Twinkies and Pop Tarts.

One of the most noticeable features of Knead is the large magnetized map of Ohio, with all 88 counties marked in different shades of reds, browns, and creams. There you'll find business cards from their

for meat, eggs, milk, vegetables, cheese, grains, greens, and more. They, in fact, were some of the earliest to draw on Ohio farms, creameries, and mills to supply their food.

Clearly they're inspiring future generations to eat better already. If you're lucky, you'll hear one of their kids - staples of the restaurant - ask for prosciutto for a snack or serve as taste-testers for new desserts.

NANCY'S HOME COOKING

3133 North High Street
Columbus, OH 43202

(614) 265-9012

"Cindy had cared for the community, and now this was the community's chance to care for her."

Nancy's Home Cooking is technically owned now by Sheila Davis-Hahn and her husband Rick, but the Clintonville neighborhood has just as much of a stake in the diner as they do.

In early 2009, owner Cindy King (Sheila's aunt) announced that, after 40 years of garbage omelets, chicken and noodles, and "Eat It & Beat It," the narrow diner space in Clintonville would be closing. The reaction by the community was little short of a riot.

There was a Nancy who started the diner in 1972, but quit after running it for two years. Cindy bought it, keeping the name because, well, it was cheaper and easier than changing it. Over forty years, she made the restaurant into a Clintonville mainstay by caring for the community. She took care of college students and neighbors. She gave homeless people meals in exchange for a little work.

When Cindy told her family about her decision, citing mounting medical bills and costs to upgrade the restaurant, most of them dediced to let it go. Except Sheila and Rick. They were prepared to move to Florida to new jobs and a new house, but Sheila felt called to re-open her aunt's restaurant.

She wasn't the only one. When Cindy announced the closing publicly, Clintonville sprang into action. A substantial amount of money was needed to repair the space and bring it up to code. So a loyal customer immediately started a "Save Nancy's Home Cooking!!!!" Facebook group. Patrick J's bar held a fundraiser night. Members from the Clintonville Chamber of Commerce "panhandled" in front of the restaurant and raised $9000 in one day. Lowe's donated a new floor. Contractors gave their time to rewire electricity, install a new furnace and air conditioning, and redo plumbing. Volunteers showed up to paint the walls. A customer who lived nearby donated his garage for space to refurbish the equipment, about 90% of which was preserved. And

the checks poured in, from in town, around the state, and even out of the country. Past customers, Ohio State alumni, old area residents, former OSU football players all contributed. The community's generosity in time, money, and resources rebuilt this institution.

Cindy had cared for the community, and now this was the community's chance to care for her. And it worked. On Friday, February 19, 2010, at 6 a.m., Rick and Sheila set out the little "Nancy's Open" sign on the sidewalk yet again.

The new space feels cleaner and brighter than the old one, but the U-shaped counters and lines of booths are still there. The "Eat It & Beat It" sign still reminds customers not to dawdle after they eat. Regulars still gather for their inexpensive plates of eggs and potatoes, the sausage gravy and biscuits, and the famous garbage omelets. Oh, and breakfast is now served all day.

TASI CAFE

680 North Pearl Street
Columbus, OH 43215

(614) 222-0788

tasicafe.com

@tasicafe

Down one of the brick side streets of Short North, on the lowest level of an apartment building with barely four parking spots out front, you'll find one of Columbus' coziest, off-the-beaten-path cafés. Initially, it was going to be called "Home," a nod to the fact that it could be your second home, a place as familiar and comfortable as your own kitchen.

Although the café ended up taking the name of its owner, the homey feeling is definitely still there. The name comes from Tasi Rigsby, married to Kent, owner of Short North mainstay Rigsby's Kitchen. The Rigsbys know the neighborhood well. When Short North was still considered a dangerous place twenty-five years ago, Kent took a chance to open an upscale restaurant there. His lead helped drive the revitalization of the neighborhood, and now the area is a nationally-recognized arts district.

> "Initially, it was going to be called "Home," a nod to the fact that it could be your second home, a place as familiar and comfortable as your own kitchen."

They've established their presence in the neighborhood. Down another side street is their bakery, Elena Christina, which creates spectacular breads for their restaurants and many others. Next to the café, they recently opened a gallery called Ray's Living Room. So when a small patisserie called Pistachio decided to move their operation from Pearl Alley to German Village (and rename themselves Pistacia Vera), they let the Rigsbys know the space was becoming available right away. Tasi had always wanted to open a café, a place serving

a solid and comfortable breakfast. So, they took the space and opened it in November 2007 on the night of Gallery Hop.

Tasi, who grew up in Greece, planned an eclectic menu and space that reflects her personality. Her favorite color, for instance, is red. So you'll see dashes of it in the chairs, coffee mugs, shirts, and more. These stand out from the brick walls, the big wooden communal table, the intricate glassware, and the long counters.

And Tasi's goal of creating a cozy cafe with enticing comfort food has been achieved. Short North regulars and visitors alike turn to the cafe for breakfasts like poached eggs on black bean cakes, cinnamon challah French toast (with bread made in the bakery), or smoked salmon bagel sandwiches. There are some Greek touches, too, like Greek Scrambled Eggs, with feta, tomato, and zucchini, or Greek yogurt with honey and granola. You can always keep it simple with an espresso and one of their delectable croissants.

TIP TOP KITCHEN & COCKTAILS

73 East Gay Street
Columbus, OH 43215

(614) 221-8300

tiptopcolumbus.com

@tiptopkitchen

The short section of Gay Street between High Street and Third Avenue is proof that Columbus' downtown is on the upswing. At the center of that is the cozy, pub-like Tip Top Kitchen & Cocktails. Tip Top is just one of the (currently) five members of the Columbus Food League. It was the third to join the family, opening in spring of 2007 on burgeoning Gay Street, which has since seen more restaurants and shops and street vendors. Tip Top's focus, aside from doing a great brunch, is its celebration of all things Columbus and Ohio. You'll see cardinals adorning the bar shelves. The walls are loaded with pieces of Columbus history: photos of former rock bands, signed pictures of old mayors, Columbus Police Department files, and faded postcards featuring the LeVeque Tower. Much of the paraphernalia was donated by the Ohio Historical Society. The low lighting almost covers the mix of old downtown building décor and the lovingly tacky details. Exposed brick walls and a dark tin ceiling mix with old curtains and faded chandeliers. The shelves of the wooden bar are also filled with knick-knacks and bottles of spirits.

"Tip Top's focus, aside from doing a great brunch, is its celebration of all things Columbus and Ohio."

This, says general manager Tim Lessner, is what makes a "tipsy downtown neighborhood whiskey bar." Just as the walls boast Ohio history, the weekend brunch menu features Ohio comfort foods like apple cinnamon pancakes, breakfast burritos, and omelets loaded with Ohio vegetables. Customers flock all week long for Tip Top's Blue Ribbon pot roast; one mention of the sandwich online entices a wave of downtown workers in for lunch. The breakfast version uses the spicy pot roast as a base for a skillet, covered with potatoes, scrambled eggs, and veggies. If meat isn't your choice, Tip Top (and all the CFL restaurants) offer plenty of vegetarian and vegan dishes. One of your best bets at Tip Top's brunch is their sweet potato hash, mixed with black-eyed peas, onions, peppers, and herbs.

Where does Tip Top get it's name? It's a nod to a further bit of Columbus history. Back in the 1950's, Bob Marvin took to the airwaves at WBNS as Flippo, King of the Clowns. Beginning with his show, "Flippo the Clown and the Tip-Top Bandwagon," he reigned the Columbus airwaves for over 30 years. Now, a small part of his fun-loving heritage lives on in this downtown neighborhood bar.

ZENCHA TEA SALON

982 North High Street
Columbus, OH 43201

(614) 421-2140

zen-cha.com

@zenchateasalon

Tea is the name of the game at ZenCha Tea Salon. And it's everywhere, not just in your cup: in the pancakes, in the syrup, in the waffles.

Jean Wu and I-Cheng Huang opened their first ZenCha in Short North in 2002. Their intent was to create a haven where customers could experience tea truly as a time to pause in life. The interior of the restaurant emphasizes an atmosphere of comfort and relaxation. The space is decorated in soft and warm colors like cream and yellow and brown. Bright green stalks of bamboo grow in the front windows.

ZenCha is the place to go to learn about tea. They feature tea from all over the world. Just look at the categories listed in their menu: China, Taiwan, Japan, India, Great Britain, Germany, the Middle East, Africa, and South America. They serve many different types of tea as well: green, black, white, dark, herbal, Roobios (a South African red tea), and oolong (a Chinese tea that is sun-dried and rolled into balls). ZenCha also supplies tea and brewing equipment; their "Tea Ambassadors" will gladly teach you how to bring the tea experience home.

"ZenCha is the place to go to learn about tea."

Many of their weekend brunch menu items are as complex as the tea itself. Expect layer upon layer of flavors and ingredients, mixing flavors from both eastern and western cultures. For instance, how about masala waffles? Made with a chai spice batter, they're topped with banana, mango, and whipped cream. Or the red pepper basil strata, a casserole-like dish layered with red bell peppers, goat and parmesan cheeses, and turkey bacon. One of the big draws, however, is the tea pancakes. Options for these fluffy creations range from sweet to savory and are filled with all manner of surprising ingredients. The Earl Grey's Choice pancakes are infused with earl grey tea in the batter, then topped with baked apples, raisins,

and walnuts. You can douse them with a house-made earl grey tea syrup. On the savory side are the Okonomiyaki, which are savory pancakes served with your choice of chicken, seafood, or vegetables, then covered with shitake mushrooms, cabbage, and onions, and drizzled with mayo and yaki sauce (think of a variation on Worcestershire sauce). Other items, like traditional blueberry pancakes, hash browns, or eggs in a basket, round out a peaceful and intricate breakfast experience.

AU BON PAIN

20 South Third Street
Columbus, OH 43215
(614) 224-1922
aubonpain.com
@aubonpain

This is the single Columbus location of the international chain, situated across the street from the Ohio Statehouse. The breakfast is meant for weekday grab-and-go customers, and features sandwiches made with bagels or ciabatta bread, oatmeal, yogurt with fruit, plus the full gamut of coffee drinks and smoothies.

AUDDINO'S ITALIAN BAKERY

1490 Clara Street
Columbus, OH 43211
(614) 294-2577

You may see the Auddino's truck around town, delivering their Italian goods to all the groceries and restaurants, but it's well worth discovering their side street, looks-like-a-warehouse bakery. The Auddino family - mom, dad, and the kids - serve up some delightful donuts, including their glazed croissants, custard-filled longjohns, cake and sour cream donuts, and their elusive lobster tails.

BARRIO

185 North High Street
Columbus, OH 43215
(614) 220-9141
barriotapas.com
@barriotapas

Barrio's Latin American menu translates into a wicked weekend brunch: try arepas made with spicy strawberries, caramelized bacon, and maple syrup. Or there's huevos rellenos, essentially breakfast burrito ingredients stuffed into a poblano pepper. Other items include chilaquiles, tostadas, and a spicy burger.

BETTY'S FINE FOOD & SPIRITS

680 North High Street
Columbus, OH 43215
(614) 228-6191
bettyscolumbus.com
@bettyscolumbus

The first of the Columbus Food League (formerly called the Betty's Family of Restaurants), Betty's is a one-room eatery in the heart of Short North, decorated with pin-up girls and sporting a general sassy attitude. Weekend brunch favorites include omelets like the Mean Drunk, with spicy eggs, veggies, poblano peppers, and hot sauce. In addition to more brunch classics, many other dishes have a Mexican feel, like quesadillas, huevos rancheros, or the Never Again Nachos, with blue corn chips, beans, eggs, cheese, and veggies.

BIG BITE

79 South Fourth Street
Columbus, OH 43215
(614) 358-0615

A newcomer to the downtown breakfast scene, Big Bite keeps customers fueled with sandwiches and wraps, French toast and pancakes, plus omelets, home fries, toast, and bacon.

BLUE DANUBE

2439 North High Street
Columbus, OH 43202
(614) 261-9308

The Dube is a dive bar favorite with Ohio State students, located just north of campus. Relax on the weekend with cheap mimosas, giant breakfast burritos, omelets, or eggs benedict. Whether sitting in a booth or at the bar, be sure to check out the ceiling tiles, all colorfully decorated by locals.

CAFE BRIOSO

14 East Gay Street #1
Columbus, OH 43215
(614) 228-8366
cafebrioso.com
@cafebrioso

Cafe Brioso is a downtown mecca for coffee lovers. You can smell roasting coffee up and down the city streets when roastmaster Jeff Davis is at work. Enjoy his coffee prepared by some of Columbus' best-trained baristas, and fill yourself with their freshly-made rolls, sweet and savory scones, or the popular blueberry muffins. Brioso baristas can adorn your drinks with exquisite latte art; they regularly compare their skills to regional baristas by hosting barista jams and latte art competitions.

CAFFÉ APROPOS

443 West Third Avenue
Columbus, OH 43201
(614) 294-5282
@caffeapropos

A European-style espresso bar serving house-roasted coffee drinks, bagels, and panini-grilled breakfast sandwiches. You can keep it traditional with eggs, cheese, and meat on a sandwich, or mix it up with a sandwich of Nutella, bananas, and strawberry preserves. This little corner shop, in the heart of Harrison West, is a favorite spot for industrious Ohio State graduate students and for neighbors who want to sit on the patio, sip their coffee, and read a book.

CAFFE ILLYRIA

214 East State Street
Columbus, OH 43215
(614) 227-3330

Illyria is one of many downtown restaurants clearly aimed at the weekday working crowd. Situated in the basement level of a building just a few blocks from the Statehouse, the cafe does $3-6 breakfasts of omelets, egg combos, hotcakes, and the full range of espresso, lattes, and cappuccinos.

CAPITOL CAFE BY MILO'S

1 Capitol Square
Columbus, OH 43215
(614) 728-9231
ohiostatehouse.org

If you're looking to get a good start on a day of downtown sightseeing, you can start right at the center of Ohio's government. In the basement of the Ohio Statehouse, amongst vaulted brick ceilings and historical displays, Capitol Cafe serves simple and inexpensive breakfasts of eggs, omelets, burritos, and pancakes. Owner Louie Pappas draws on his tried-and-true experience working at family-owned Milo's Deli and Tommy's Diner in Franklinton.

CASA SAZON

49 North High Street
Columbus, OH 43215
(614) 221-8311

A little Latin Deli on High Street downtown, Casa Sazon's breakfast focuses on American fare like sandwiches, wraps, and burritos. Aside from the easy to-go options, there are plates of pancakes or platters of eggs, meat, and hash browns.

CORNERSTONE DELI & CAFE

3296 North High Street
Columbus, OH 43202
(614) 267-3354
@cornerstonedeli

Cornerstone is a much-loved Clintonville restaurant that serves an eclectic mix of foods. Breakfast fare includes coffee, bagels, sandwiches, and wraps.

CRIMSON CUP COFFEE HOUSE

4541 North High Street
Columbus, OH 43214
(614) 262-6212
crimsoncup.com
@crimsoncup

Crimson Cup is a very active roaster, and their coffee can be found all over the city, but they do have this one dedicated coffee shop up in northern Clintonville. Here they serve their roasts to studying students, the business crowd holding meetings, and folks in the drive-through.

DANNY'S DELI & RESTAURANT.

37 West Broad Street
Columbus, OH 43215
(614) 469-7040
dannysdeli.net

Danny's makes a big deal out of their corned beef, so it's no surprise that their breakfast menu, served weekday mornings, features omelets, sandwiches, hash, and egg specials with it. If the beef isn't your thing, try pancakes, French toast, or a healthy breakfast of egg whites, steamed potatoes, turkey, and onions. To find Danny's, look for the red awning on the west side of the Huntington Building downtown.

DE-NOVO BISTRO & BAR

201 South High Street
Columbus, OH 43215
(614) 496-1002

de-NOVO recently joined the ranks of downtown eating. Situated across from the Columbus Commons, the restaurant serves creative breakfasts like creme brulee French toast, eggs benedicts with crab or salmon, or mushroom and truffle omelets.

DIRTY FRANK'S HOT DOG PALACE

248 South Fourth Street
Columbus, Oh 43215
(614) 824-4673
dirtyfrankscolumbus.com
@dirtyfranksdogs

As Columbus' premiere hot dog stop, Dirty Frank's has drawn a lot of national attention for its creative toppings and kooky menu. It was the last of the Columbus Food League restaurants to add weekend brunch to its menu. Now, finally, you can enjoy an Ohio Scramble of eggs, cheese, corn relish, and chips... topped with sliced hot dogs. The menu also features breakfast nachos, French toast sticks, vegan scrambles, and funky cocktails.

DRAGONFLY NEO-V

247 King Avenue
Columbus, OH 43201
(614) 298-9986
dragonflyneov.com
@dragonflyneov

This award-winning upscale vegan eatery does a Saturday brunch, too! Enjoy wine or cocktails with a continental buffet of pastries and salad, then choose an entree from selections like mushroom risotto, pancakes, omelets, or even macaroni and cheese.

EGGFAST

24 East Twelfth Avenue
Columbus, OH 43201
(614) 294-3447
eggfast.com
@eggfast_

It's breakfast made especially for the late night, on-the-go college crowd. Twenty-four hours a day, you can visit Eggfast's small dining room just across from Ohio State's campus, or you can order delivery online. Foods are made for the move: versions of hash brown casserole, flatbread, and Tex-Mex eggs migas (combines scrambled eggs and tortilla strips).

GARCIA'S INTERNAZIONALE

2573 North High Street
Columbus, OH 43202
(614) 268-4888
garcias-restaurant.com

At 35 years old, Garcia's is one of Columbus' oldest running Mexican restaurants, tucked into Old North Columbus with a small, colorful storefront. Their weekend breakfast is served overnight from 12 am to 6 am (you read that right). The menu includes eggs, pancakes, omelets, and French toast, plus a few specialties like the Breakfast Pizza and the Hudson Street Breakfast Burrito.

GLOBAL GALLERY COFFEE SHOP

3535 North High Street
Columbus, OH 43214
(614) 262-5535
globalgalleryonline.org
@globalgallery

Global Gallery is your coffee shop with a conscience. Their store in the heart of Clintonville sells coffee, tea, and snacks, all procured by fair trade methods. While enjoying their fare, be sure to shop through the selection of fair trade goods like clothes, jewelry, and toys.

GORDON'S GOURMET

150 East Gay Street
Columbus, OH 43215
(614) 224-0911
gordonsgourmetofcolumbus.com

Gordon's recently moved from Grandview to a downtown location at the corner of Fourth and Gay Streets. Owned by an accomplished Columbus chef, Gordon's serves a weekday breakfast of croissant sandwiches, meat and veggie burritos, and parfaits. Breakfast is easily taken to-go, or you can enjoy it in the cafe or on their outdoor seating.

HANGOVER EASY

1646 Neil Avenue
Columbus, OH 43201
(614) 586-0070
hangovereasy.com
@hangovereasy

This colorful campus-area favorite is tucked in a small storefront on Neil Avenue, across from the Ohio State Medical Center. Breakfast dishes sport fun names like the Ramblin Man (French toast, eggs, potatoes, toast), the New Amsterdam (a Belgian waffle), or the Fat Joe's (2 pancakes, 2 eggs, 2 choices of meat, potatoes, and toast). Potatoes are served as "hoe fries," meaning "hang over easy," which basically means home fries with lots of pepper.

HEIRLOOM

1871 North High Street
Columbus, OH 43210
(614) 292-3535
wexarts.org/info/cafe

This tiny cafe sits in the lower floor of the award-winning Wexner Center for the Arts on Ohio State's campus. The menu focuses on using local ingredients. Take a break from wandering the galleries to enjoy Stauf's coffee, some homemade muffins, a breakfast burrito, or yogurt and granola.

HIGH STREET GRILL

310 South High Street
Columbus, OH 43215
(614) 220-7007
hsgrill.com

You don't have to be staying at the beautiful Westin Hotel downtown to eat breakfast there. Enjoy the continental or full breakfast buffet; order up some blueberry orange pancakes or spicy turkey soft breakfast tacos; keep healthy with muesli or a parfait.

IMPERO COFFEE

849 North High Street
Columbus, OH 43215
(614) 294-2489
imperocoffee.com
@imperocoffee

This Short North coffee roaster and cafe can be found in the newer Dakota building. Stop in for exquisitely roasted and prepared espressos, cubanos, French presses, and pour overs.

BREAKFAST AT THE NORTH MARKET

59 Spruce Street, Columbus, OH 43215 | northmarket.com | @northmarket

The North Market is already a required stop for anyone exploring Columbus' culinary scene. Not only does the market offer a taste of cuisines from around the world, but it serves your basic grocery store needs as well: fruits and vegetables, bread and pastries, fish and poultry. On top of that, it operates as an incubator for many small businesses: Thang Nguyen's Lac Viet got its start there, pretzel-makers from brezel established their permanent location there, and Columbus culinary celebrity Jeni Britton Bauer first made her splendid ice creams there.

You can stroll your way through the market for breakfast, too. Just about every day you'll find the basics: coffee, pastries, and small snacks. If you want a bigger meal, head in on the weekends (especially Saturdays), and here's what you'll find:

The most substantial breakfast offerings are created at Kitchen Little. Dan, AnneMarie, and Jerry cook up ultimate comfort food breakfasts. An extension of North Market Poultry & Game, Kitchen Little draws on local meats and eggs to create succulent dishes like baked French toast, biscuits with a sweet chicken sausage gravy, duck fat fries, breakfast sliders, and their Cuban breakfast: eggs, black beans, pico de gallo, avocado, smoked turkey, and fried plantains.

Stroll across the aisle from Kitchen Little to Taste of Belgium, serving up Liege-style Belgian waffles. These hand-held treats are made with beet sugar infused in the batter, resulting in a dense, caramelized waffle that's nothing like what you'd expect. Taste of Belgium also makes sweet and savory crepes, and offers coffee drinks.

Down the aisle, Bubbles offers freshly squeezed juices, smoothies, and teas in convenient to-go containers. A Touch of Earth serves up fresh tea and Stauf's coffee; you can also purchase whole beans. Best of the Wurst serves breakfast wraps, biscuits, and French toast sandwiches, while nationally-recognized Clever Crow Pizza has started serving up breakfast pizzas.

Dominating the southwest corner of the Market is Omega Artisan Bakery. Since starting in 2003, proprietor Amy Lozier has served long lines of customers hoping to snag fresh breads, croissants, and scones oozing with berries. Their cinnamon rolls were even named the Best Breakfast in Ohio by *Food Network Magazine!*

On the east side of the Market, Expressly Market Bakery & Bistro offers coffee, simple pastries, and breakfast quiches. Look to them for vegan and vegetarian items, too! Finally, if you're nabbing supplies to make breakfast at home, you can pick up farm fresh eggs, Snowville Creamery milk, or Stutzman Farms granola at The Greener Grocer.

JACK & BENNY'S

2563 North High Street
Columbus, OH 43202
(614) 263-0242
jackandbennys.com
@jackbennysdiner

Jack and Benny's shows up on every must-visit list for Ohio State students. The simple, old diner space, with stumpy counter stools and a polished wooden floor, is adorned with old coffee mugs, pictures of past OSU football teams, and a display case full of OSU bobbleheads. On gamedays and weekends, you'll see a small crowd gathered outside. They're lining up for inexpensive breakfasts of Buckeye pancakes, huge omelets, or any of the all-inclusive Busters. Try the Gutbuster, for instance, loaded with a potato pancake, hash browns, sausage, ham, an egg, and cheese, then covered in gravy.

JAVA JAN GOURMET COFFEE

175 On the Park
Columbus, OH 43215
(614) 824-1177
javajangourmetcoffee.com
@javajancoffee

The second location of the Dublin-based coffee shop, recently opened on the Columbus Commons. Enjoy all of your coffee drinks - espresso, cappuccino, tea, and smoothies - as well as items like breakfast sandwiches, gourmet muffins, bagels, pastries, yogurt, and quiches.

JURY ROOM

22 East Mound Street
Columbus, OH 43215
(614) 220-0964
juryroomcolumbus.com
@jury_room

As Columbus' oldest continually operating restaurant (begun in 1831!), the Jury Room was reborn in recent years as a member of the Columbus Food League. The eatery takes its name from its proximity to the Franklin County Courthouse. Their weekend brunch features goodies like breakfast hoagies, flatbreads, brioche French toast, and frittatas, topped off with coffee and cocktails.

KAFE KEROUAC

2250 North High Street
Columbus, OH 43201
(614) 299-2672
kafekerouac.com

This north campus coffee shop and bar features shelves lined with old books and a side room popular for play performances, poetry readings, and comedy shows. Favorites include standard coffee, biscotti and muffins, plus a huge menu of specialty coffee drinks named after famous authors.

LATITUDE 41

50 North Third Street
Columbus, OH 43215
(614) 233-7541
latitude41restaurant.com
@latitude41cbus

In the Renaissance Hotel downtown, you can find a hotel restaurant that clearly stands on its own. Latitude 41 does a daily breakfast featuring selected local ingredients. Enjoy a full or continental buffet on the weekends, or try succulent breakfasts like capri benedicts, steel cut Irish oatmeal, wild mushroom frittatas, chicken hash and eggs, or peanut butter and banana French toast with Nutella.

LEXI'S ON THIRD

100 East Broad Street
Columbus, OH 43215
(614) 229-5394
lexisonthird.com
@lexisonthird

A newer cafe at the bottom of the Chase building downtown, Lexi's does weekday breakfasts with a wide selection. Load up with an omelet, try the Que Pasa sandwich with sausage, eggs, salsa, jalapenos, and sour cream, or split a SoBe Breakfast Pizza with eggs, cheese, and bacon or sausage.

MARKET 65
65 East State Street
Columbus, OH 43215
(614) 564-6565
marketsixtyfive.com
@marketsixtyfive

Like a fast casual farmers' market, Market 65 serves up a wide range of custom-made salads and wraps built from local ingredients. The bright green restaurant features a small but tasty breakfast menu of super-customizable wraps, local baked goods, and Stauf's coffee. The central downtown location - close to the Statehouse and Columbus Commons - offers a quick and healthy breakfast for downtown workers or the sip-and-enjoy casual crowd.

MOUTON
954 North High Street
Columbus, OH 43215
mouton954.com
@moutononhigh

Mouton is known already as a place for great wine and cocktails, and their Sunday brunch has proved just as exquisite. Given the lack of a full kitchen, brunch at Mouton is created by hand and overall much lighter than eggs, bacon, and pancakes. Instead, revive yourself with drinks while you sample Pistacia Vera croissants, the fresh Farmer Jones' Salad, or cheese and meat trays.

MOZART'S CAFE
2885 North High Street
Columbus, OH 43202
(614) 268-3687
mozartscafe.com
@mozartscafe

This Clintonville mainstay is known for their Austrian-themed goods served in a very classy atmosphere. In addition to their vast array of beautiful pastries, you can order dishes named for their classical music theme: the Vienna Waltz omelet comes with roasted red peppers, artichokes, gouda, and seasonal veggies. Eggs Amadeus are scrambled with parmesan and zucchini. Or the Tyrolean Breakfast (named after a region of Austria) includes sautéed potatoes, black forest ham, scrambled eggs, and bacon.

NORTHSTAR CAFÉ
951 North High Street
Columbus, OH 43201
(614) 298-9999
thenorthstarcafe.com

Now one of Columbus' breakfast mainstays, Northstar Cafe originated at this Short North location. Within weeks of opening, lines of customers formed out the door and onto the sidewalk to enjoy breakfast burritos, ricotta pancakes, and mushroom fritatas. Breakfast is complemented by rich coffees, fresh-squeezed orange juice, and thick smoothies. During the warmer months, you can enjoy breakfast on their patio; there's even a water bowl for your pooch.

PATTYCAKE BAKERY
3009 North High Street
Columbus, OH 43202
(614) 784-2253
pattycakebakery.com
@pattycakebakery

A funky, favorite bakery that embodies everything to love about Clintonville. Jennie Scheinbach and her crew bake up breakfast goods of muffins, granola bars, and huge sticky buns. They feature many vegan and gluten-free options, as well!

PHILLIP'S CONEY ISLAND
747 North High Street
Columbus, OH 43215
(614) 294-1251

One of many restaurants around the country named Coney Island, this one-room shop is smack dab in the middle of Short North and still serves inexpensive made-from-scratch breakfasts.

SHORT NORTH PIECE OF CAKE
772 North High Street #104
Columbus, OH 43215
(614) 421-0399
shortnorthpieceofcake.com

On a side street in Short North, Piece of Cake gives you a calm spot to sit and watch the busy bakery workers. Enjoy a simple breakfast of coffee and a muffin, or choose a more filling option like bacon and egg tarts, savory scones, or grilled panini sandwiches.

SLOOPY'S DINER

2619 North High Street
Columbus, OH 43202
(614) 263-9650
ohiounion.osu.edu/dine_and_shop/sloopys
In the heart of Ohio State's new Ohio Union is a breakfast diner named after The McCoy's 1965 hit "Hang On Sloopy," which is one of the Ohio State Marching Band's most popular numbers. Eat breakfast off scarlet and gray plates, with scarlet and gray mugs, while sitting in scarlet and gray booths. Join students for a late night breakfast of burritos, pancakes, and skillets. Or fuel up on game day at the breakfast buffet.

SPINELLI'S DELI

767 Neil Avenue
Columbus, OH 43215
(614) 280-1044
spinellisdeli.com
@spinellisdeli
Spinelli's is one of Columbus' go-to delis, and their breakfast has kept our city fueled for years. Stop in this Victorian Village spot for a lox and cream cheese bagel, a Tostini sandwich, a croissant with eggs and Taylor ham, or sit down with a big stack of Cinnamon Crème Pancakes or a Basil Vegetable Scramble.

STAUF'S COFFEE ROASTERS

1277 Grandview Avenue
Columbus, OH 43212
(614) 486-4861
staufs.com
@staufs
Supplying the coffee to all the Cup O' Joe shops, as well as a number of Columbus restaurants, Stauf's is your go-to stop for coffee drinks and snacks, roasted whole beans, or coffee and tea equipment. Their Grandview cafe is a favorite for studying, reading, or just catching up with friends. Their new breakfast menu features prepared dishes that have included waffles, biscuits and gravy, and huevos rancheros.

SUNNY STREET CAFÉ

277 West Nationwide Boulevard
Columbus, OH 43215
(614) 222-3008
sunnystreetcafe.com
@sunnystreet_AD
The downtown location of a casual cafe chain formerly called Rise & Dine, this Sunny Street offers a comfortable breakfast of egg, meat, potato, and pancake platters, Tex-Mex Omelets, or a Breakfast Sundae that layers yogurt, granola, and fresh fruit.

SURLY GIRL SALOON

1126 North High Street
Columbus, OH 43201
(614) 294-4900
surlygirlsaloon.com
@surlygirlsaloon
If you want a little fun attitude with your breakfast, you need to hit up cowgirl-themed Surly Girl for their weekend brunch. The Sassy Sausage Gravy is spiked with chorizo; the High Noon sandwich features eggs, bacon, tomato, lettuce, and avocado; and the Chuck Wagon Pizza blends eggs, potatoes, bacon, and cheese with a rich ranchero sauce.

TRAVONNA COFFEE HOUSE

1195 North High Street
Columbus, OH 43201
(614) 725-4151
travonnacoffee.com
@travonnacoffee
Travonna is a rare coffee shop that's open twenty-four hours a day. Stop in any time for an espresso, a latte, a smoothie, or some tea. You can also begin your day with a bowl of oatmeal, sausage gravy poured over biscuits, or a breakfast sandwich.

SIDE DISH:
CUP O' JOE

Cup O' Joe is Columbus' local coffee shop. With eight locations spread around town, Cup O' Joe offers the right place for all of your needs, whether you need a quick caffeine fix, are after some study space, holding business meetings, are working from home, or just need a spot to stop and relax after shopping. They brew and serve coffee roasted by Stauf's in Grandview, and feature locally made muffins, bagels, scones, and more.

cupojoecoffee.com
@cupojoecoffee

4600 International Gateway
(Port Columbus
 International Airport)
Columbus, OH 43219
(614) 231-6563

627 South Third Street
(German Village)
Columbus, OH 43206
(614) 221-1563

1791 Olentangy River Road
(Lennox)
Columbus, OH 43212
(614) 291-1563

2990 North High Street
(Clintonville)
Columbus, OH 43202
(614) 447-7563

600 North High Street
(Short North)
Columbus, OH 43215
(614) 225-1563

149 South High Street
(Downtown)
Columbus, OH 43215
(614) 732-4899

241 Easton Town Center
(Easton)
Columbus, OH 43219
(614) 471-1563

2418 East Main Street
 (Bexley)
Columbus, OH 43209
(614) 239-6563

WAREHOUSE CAFÉ
243 North Fifth Street
Columbus, Oh 43215
(614) 224-3134
This downtown favorite breakfast is tucked into a small brick room in a former factory. Take in the beautiful walls and wooden floors while you munch on inexpensive plates of French toast, eggs and bacon, or breakfast wraps and sandwiches.

WHOLE WORLD RESTAURANT
3269 North High Street
Columbus, Oh 43202
(614) 268-5751
wholeworldnaturalrestaurant.com
@wwrestaurant
Whole World is one of your best stops for vegan and vegetarian brunching in town. Their Sunday brunch includes pancakes with fruit, vegetable hash, quiche, scrambled tofu, and even a vegetarian sausage gravy and biscuits.

WILDFLOWER CAFÉ
3420 Indianola Avenue
Columbus, OH 43214
(614) 262-2233
This tiny Clintonville eatery has a very dedicated clientele, judging by their crowded parking lot. The one-room diner has a small counter, checkered floors, and plenty of wildflower decorations. Order up classic breakfasts of omelets, French toast, or eggs with home fries and bacon.

YEAH, ME TOO
3005 Indianola Avenue
Columbus, OH 43202
No phone number, no website, no Facebook page. Just amazing coffee. Jovan and Sam roast beans and serve French-pressed goodness out of this one-room Clintonville operation. Look for the tiny, tiny blue building with the big yellow "Coffee" letters. View local art on the walls, pick up some local baked goods, and enjoy some of Columbus' best coffee.

SOUTHWEST

FRANKLINTON, HILLTOP, SOUTH SIDE, GROVE CITY

Columbus' southwest corner includes many restaurants that invite you to trek out to undiscovered country. Visit classic diners in Franklinton, a neighborhood coming back to life as an arts district, just west of downtown. Trek on down to Grove City and stroll along Broadway after you eat breakfast. Travel down the southern reaches of Columbus' central corridor, High Street, to find our oldest drive-in and some classic donuts. Explore the Brewery District for coffee shops and a breakfast with loads of seafood. Or check out West Broad Street and the Mexican eats in the area. And keep your eyes peeled: the southwest section of town is packed with old greasy spoons tucked in and amongst the neighborhoods.

COYOTE JANE

340 Greenlawn Avenue
Columbus, OH 43223

(614) 824-1820

If you want to know what Chef Robin Emrick likes for breakfast, just browse the brunch menu at Coyote Jane. She's always been a big seafood person, but just couldn't find good seafood breakfast dishes around Columbus, in particular a seafood version of an eggs benedict. Her answer: start a restaurant that served the food she wanted. And the first dish she created was the Keys Poacher: smoked salmon and poached eggs, served over biscuits with a side of grits.

"No one else was serving heaping piles of Bananas Foster French Toast or Eggs del Mar."

Coyote Jane is now home to the Banana Bean Cafe, a name that's instantly recognizable to regulars in the Columbus dining scene. Robin combined the two concepts in the space formerly occupied by Banana Bean in the Brewery District. There are new menu additions and subtractions (the Keys Poacher comes and goes, for instance) and the decor has changed slightly, but the favorites are all there.

Banana Bean itself started in a small German Village space on Whittier Avenue, and quickly became popular for its inventive weekend brunch menu. No one else was serving heaping piles of Bananas Foster French Toast or Eggs del Mar. Robin created the concept and started the restaurant with her sister Angela in late 2005. She targeted the brunch crowd in German Village, noticing a lack of good Sunday morning meals in the neighborhood.

With only nine tables and a steady stream of customers, Robin decided to move the restaurant west to the Brewery District in 2008. The new space features more dining areas, a big stone fireplace, a long bar, soft colors and music, with touches of both Key West and the Southwest.

Just reading the menu descriptions should be enough to bring you in. The Cedar Key Shrimp & Grits are made with a smoked bacon étoufée. The Eggs del Mar layer poached eggs, crabcakes, spinach, and hollandaise. Omelets are made with andouille, crimini mushrooms, or enchilada ingredients. There's Lobster Hash and espresso-rubbed steak, plus a dish pairing fried chicken, eggs, biscuits, and sausage gravy. Roasted Corn and Blueberry Pancakes feature, well, you get the idea. The journey of Banana Bean and Coyote Jane continues, and Chef Robin is sure to make it a flavorful one.

LA PLAZA TAPATIA

4233 Shoppers Lane
Columbus, OH 43228

(614) 276-0333

laplazatapatiaoh.com

@laplazaohio

"Breakfast - *desayunos* - is served every day."

Fans of the popular taco trucks in Columbus will already be familiar with the location of La Plaza Tapatia. The Mexican market and restaurant is situated near the intersection of Georgesville Road and West Broad Street, in and amongst some of the best Mexican and Honduran food trucks in town.

The store takes its name from a plaza in Guadalajara, Mexico. La Plaza is a full supermarket: there are fresh homemade pastries, a full butcher's shop (including house-made chorizo sausage), produce, prepared foods, and basic grocery items. If you're looking to prepare an authentic Mexican dish at home, or seeking out some hard-to-find items, it's worth taking a stroll through the market aisles. To make your own continental-style breakfast, pair a cup of coffee with one of the pastries, especially the *pan dulce*, a giant, lightly sweet and puffy pastry that looks like an over-sized clam shell.

Breakfast - *desayunos* - is served every day, including a buffet on weekday mornings; you can sample everything from the buffet or order à la carte. If you're relatively new to authentic Mexican food, you'll still find familiar dishes like omelets, burritos, quesadillas, chiles rell.eños, and taco salad on the menu. You also have the option of scrambled or fried eggs mixed with different meats. One colorful and flavorful dish is huevos divorciados (literally, "divorced eggs"), which are two fried eggs, one prepared in a red (roja) sauce and and one in a green (verde) sauce. Chilaquiles, meanwhile, feature a thin strip steak from the market's butcher, seared and served over corn tortilla slices and eggs, simmered in a roja or verde sauce, and lightly coated with cream and a white cheese. Most dishes are served with sides of rice, cheese, and refried beans, and are complemented by a variety of juices and smoothies, featuring banana and papaya.

The buffet offers an incredible variety of foods, from eggs with jalapeños to chicken in mole and verde sauces. (Mole is a rich, dark sauce made with chocolate and spicy peppers.) Try tortilla soup, gorditas, chilaquiles, and huevos campesinos. Top off everything with a mix of salsas and seasonings, and be sure to leave room for desserts like sweet potatoes and sopapillas (fried bread).

The entire menu is in Spanish, but if you're not a Spanish-speaker, don't let that intimidate you. The staff at La Plaza are very helpful and welcoming. Here's a basic primer to help you order:

arroz. rice
asada. steak
cebolla. onion
champiñones. mushrooms
chorizo. spicy sausage
frijoles. beans
huevos. eggs (*huevos revueltos* are scrambled; *huevos estrellados* are fried sunny side up)
jamon. ham
lechuga. lettuce
pollo. chicken
queso. cheese
roja. red, usually meaning a red sauce
sopes. a dish consisting of a fried corn base, topped with cheese, meat, vegetables, & beans
tomate. tomato
tortilla de maiz frita. fried corn tortilla
tortilla harina. flour tortilla
verde. green, usually meaning a green sauce

OHIO DELI & RESTAURANT

3444 South High Street
Columbus, OH 43207

(614) 497-0577

Far down on South High Street, almost to the bottom of the I-270 loop, is a little green and white restaurant that's actually drawn some national attention. Ohio Deli is Columbus' south side option for a small, familiar restaurant that serves all the breakfast and lunch goods. Owner Eric Hejduk started the restaurant in February of 1996, importing the concept from a chain in Cleveland. He adapted the concept to fit Columbus better, revamping the breakfast menu and adding more comfort food.

Columbus food fans have long known and experienced the Deli's Dagwood Challenge, in which a diner must eat the massive deli sandwich, plus a mounded plate of fries, in thirty minutes or less. The walls of the Deli are lined with polaroids of past winners, all grinning sickeningly while holding their hard-won T-shirts. After a group of ColumbusUnderground.com members posted a video of their mass attempt at the challenge online, it drew the attention of producers from Travel Channel's *Man v. Food*. Host Adam Richman visited the Deli very early in the life of the show. It was for their second aired episode, and when producers first made contact with Eric, they didn't even have

"You don't have to eat like Adam Richman when you visit the Deli, but the portions will fill you just the same."

a name for the show yet. In September 2008, the week before the show's filming, Columbus was hit by a windstorm courtesy of Hurricane Ike. The storm knocked out power at the restaurant for four days. By that Friday, it came back on, so Eric and his crew raced to clean the restaurant and restock food. They opened just in time for that Sunday morning, when Richman and the camera crew arrived.

You don't have to eat like Adam Richman when you visit the Deli, but the portions will fill you just the same. Customers favor the skillets in particular. The Country Skillet packs in home fries, eggs, sausage, and veggies. The Cajun Skillet serves up eggs, sausage, banana peppers, tomatoes, and pepper jack cheese over a bed of soft home fries, with a side of warm biscuits. Other customers go for the Ohio Combo, which offers your choice of pancakes or French toast, plus eggs and meat. One of the more unique names on the menu are the

Spinners, which are essentially breakfast burritos. You can order Buckeye, Cajun, or Western versions; customers seem to love the Meat Lovers, packing three types of meat with cheese and eggs in the tortilla. Whatever you order, and how ever much you're in the mood for eating, Eric and his crew at the Ohio Deli have you covered.

TOMMY'S DINER

914 West Broad Street
Columbus, OH 43222

(614) 224-2422

tommyscolumbus.com

Tommy Pappas doesn't have an office. His office is the stools, the booths, and the chair behind the cash register at his diner.

Amidst the noisy clatter of the kitchen and the conversation between patrons, Tommy sits in his office and chats with his customers. He's familiar with their lives, with what they like to eat. He can start their order the minute they walk in the door. He's so involved with his customers, he can't get away from them. When he travels, he says, he's almost guaranteed to meet one of his customers while abroad.

Tommy's is the most diner-ish diner in town: neon lights, checkered floor, gleaming chrome, street signs, pictures of cars, posters of James Dean,

> ## "Tommy thinks he's still working toward landmark status, but anyone who's eaten at his restaurant even once will tell you he's already there."

Elvis, and Marilyn Monroe. And his personality runs through it all. A very prominent wall, visible once you step in the door, features pictures of him with governors, mayors, TV celebrities, and athletes. He brags how the hosts of national morning talk shows visit his diner when they come to Columbus.

He understands the value of hard work. "Whatever you do, you gotta put time into it," he'll tell you. Nothing comes easy. He himself came to the U.S. on September 11, 1977 with his wife and family. They came for the opportunities, following an aunt who owned a restaurant in Boston. Tommy eventually found himself in Columbus, working for Jolly Pirate Donuts. The owner there mentored him, teaching

the him ins and outs of business, most importantly how to keep the books. Tommy always knew he wanted to "do something big," and one day he found a 75-year-old building in Franklinton that had been a drive-in for decades. He took it over in 1989 and opened a diner under his name.

Tommy's customers have been completely loyal ever since. In November 1998, on a busy Saturday morning, a fire in the kitchen set the whole restaurant ablaze. Customers calmly pulled pictures and decorations off the walls, gathered outside, then waited to pay Tommy for their breakfast before they left. After some clean-up and renovation, the diner opened its doors again the following July, and Tommy's customers returned like nothing had happened.

Earlier in the life of the diner, Tommy considered expanding and creating more Tommy's around Columbus. He was stayed by Doral Chenowith, the infamous Grumpy Gourmet, food critic for the *Dispatch*. Chenowith argued against opening more Tommy's locations, encouraging Tommy not to mess up a good thing. Stick with what you do well, he said, "and I will make you a landmark." Tommy thinks he's still working toward landmark status, but anyone who's eaten at his restaurant even once will tell you he's already there.

EXTRA HELPINGS

ARI'S DINER

1425 Frank Road
Columbus, OH 43223
(614) 274-7747

Ari's is a small red brick diner on Columbus' southwest side. Inside you'll find Ari and Neta Poska, who have been making their customers happy since 2007 with steak and eggs, breakfast gyros, pig omelets with ham, bacon, and sausage, and specials of two eggs, meat, biscuits and gravy, and home fries.

BACKSTAGE BISTRO

503 South Front Street
Columbus, OH 43215
(614) 265-7625
sbxbackstagebistro.com
@bkstagebistro

The coffee shop and cafe of Shadowbox Live's new Brewery District performance space. Opens early every morning to serve coffee and tea drinks, local goods like Block's Bagels and Angry Baker pastries, plus fruit and yogurt.

BREAKFAST BARN

1275 Brown Road
Columbus, OH 43223
(614) 308-0173

What's not to love about this restaurant's name? Although not an actual barn, this quintessential hole in the wall embodies everything to love about diners: friendly service, cheap prices, and huge portions of all the breakfast classics, like omelets, silver dollar pancakes, and platters of country breakfasts. They also offer delivery service!

BUCKEYE DONUTS

1363 South High Street
Columbus, OH 43207
(614) 443-7470

Spreading some donut love to the south side, this off-shoot of the popular campus-area donut joint, although not officially affiliated now, opened in 1978. It serves long-time regulars twenty-four hours a day. Favorite donuts include longjohn, glazed, vanilla cream, and chocolate iced.

DAN'S DRIVE-IN

1881 South High Street
Columbus, OH 43207
(614) 444-7590

Originally Columbus' first drive-in downtown, Dan's eventually set up shop further down South High Street. In recent years, owners refurbished it to its original 1950's look. Everything gleams with shiny chrome, from the counter shelves to funky ceiling fans to the stools and booths. Step back to yesteryear with their full breakfast menu.

EXPLORERS CLUB

1586 South High Street
Columbus, OH 43207
(614) 725-0155
explorersclubmv.com

A brand new eatery with a bit of history, Explorers Club marks the return of restaurateurs Ricky Barnes and Tracy Studer to the Columbus dining scene. As the name indicates, you're invited to explore the cuisine of Cuba and the American southwest. Visit for weekend brunch and dine on chilaquiles with chorizo, Cuban French toast, a relleño omelet, or a breakfast burrito.

SMALL BATCH COFFEE ROASTERS

Who says you have to go to a coffee shop to get your caffeine fix? You can easily make your own coffee at home, using beans provided by smaller roasters. Jason Valentine of *Thunderkiss Coffee*, for instance, roasts five-pound batches in his home using equipment purchased from an old coffee shop. Jason sources his own beans, then experiments with different roasts and preparations. His passion for the fine art of coffee has translated into a flourishing small business. To find out more about Jason's operation, or how to purchase his coffee, visit thunderkisscoffee.tumblr.com.

Backroom Coffee Roasters takes their name from their back room location in the Trek Bicycle Store in Upper Arlington. They create a dozen different roasts, which are available in local stores or by delivery. Based from their bike shop location, they deliver their beans by bicycle. Their roasts are wholesaled and can be privately labeled for fundraisers. Learn where to find their beans or read more about their roasts at backroomcoffeeroasters.com.

GARDEN CAFE
4057 Broadway
Grove City, OH 43123
(614) 875-2233
Garden Cafe joined downtown Grove City's little breakfast scene in late 2010. They serve hot and cold drinks like coffee, tea, and smoothies, plus a breakfast of Belgian waffles, omelets, and egg platters. Also available are easy to carry items like bagels, sandwiches, and wraps.

JOLLY PIRATE DONUTS
3118 Southwest Boulevard
Grove City, OH 43123
(614) 871-1070
The Grove City location of an old central Ohio chain of donut shops. Only a few are left in town, but customers still flock to the yellow-lettered sign for 40 varieties of hand-made donuts and inexpensive coffee.

LILLY'S KITCHEN TABLE
4008 Broadway
Grove City, OH 43123
(614) 801-0771
Lilly's is a little mom-and-pop set up in the heart of "downtown" Grove City. Their little shop serves comfort food breakfasts like big platters, stuffed French toast, and homemade sausage gravy.

MEL'S KITCHEN
3590 Trabue Road
Columbus, OH 43204
(614) 488-6359
Stepping into Mel's Kitchen is like actually stepping into Mel's kitchen. In her one-room restaurant, Mel serves a standard Monday through Friday menu of eggs, French toast, pancakes, omelets, and egg sandwiches. On the weekends, her regulars fill up the counter seats for blintzes, crème brûlée French toast, and Mel's Gut Buster.

MILO'S DELI & CAFE

980 West Broad Street
Columbus, OH 43222
(614) 224-0104
milosdeli.com
@miloscatering

Milo's is Franklinton's deli. The West Broad Street institution is owned by the same family as Tommy's Diner (see feature) and the Capitol Cafe. Milo's serves up breakfast classics like omelets, breakfast pitas, and lox and eggs.

OLD TRAIL INN

77 South Grener Avenue
Columbus, OH 43228
(614) 878-9315

Old Trail Inn is a bar and grill that's been around for decades. They serve breakfast all day, every day. Sit up at the bar, or grab a booth and enjoy BLT sandwiches, French toast, or a six-ounce strip steak with eggs, toast, and home fries.

SHADES RESTAURANT

2486 South High Street
Columbus, OH 43207
(614) 444-6985

Shades opened in 1954 as the Three Trees, and the Shades family bought it and renamed it Shades Good Food in 1967. All that time, its rustic feel has drawn regulars for western omelets, pancakes, and grits. Sit at the counter and watch the kitchen at work, making their favorite breakfast of two eggs, meat, home fries, toast, and coffee, all for $5.

SUNNY STREET CAFÉ

2788 London Groveport Road
Grove City, OH 43123
(614) 539-0899
sunnystreetcafe.com

This is Grove City's location of a casual cafe chain. Breakfast is served all day, with an expansive menu of chicken fried steak, Denver omelets, and breakfast wraps. They serve up some harder to find items, too, like whole grain pancakes or crunchy French toast rolled in granola, coconut, and brown sugar.

TEE JAYE'S COUNTRY PLACE

4048 West Broad Street
Columbus, OH 43228
(614) 274-1374
barnyardbuster.com
@teejayes

1880 Stringtown Road
Grove City, OH 43123
(614) 871-2596

There are two locations of the central Ohio country cooking chain in the southeast part of town, one on West Broad and one in Grove City. Breakfast is served any time, twenty-four hours a day. Order up some mush, a Haystack of biscuits, eggs, cheese, and gravy, or a Country Ham and Corncake special.

BRUNCH

Columbus is a brunching city. Our favorite eateries are packed on Saturdays and Sundays with everyone from hungover hipsters to college students spending the weekend with Mom and Dad. Brunch is that wonderful meal that combines the best of both worlds. If you're an eggs and bacon person, you're covered. If you're the pasta and burgers type, you're still in good company. Columbus' brunch offerings run the gamut from super traditional to kooky and innovative.

For example, *Due Amici* exemplifies the modern brunch in Columbus. The downtown Italian restaurant welcomes weekend visitors with a relaxing vibe. You can sit up at the bar, enjoy a table in their bright, brick-walled dining room, or even enjoy a spot on the patio. The Due brunch menu features Italian favorites like beef carpaggio and antipasto for two, as well as breakfast classics such as eggs benedict and frangelica French toast. Their most unique brunch features include the Due Brunch Burger, a half pound of black angus on an English muffin with egg, bacon, cheese, and all the fixings. You can also order your breakfast in pizza form. The Breakfast Pizza layers bacon, sausage, cheese, and tomatoes, and tops it with a fried egg for dipping. Brunch at Due Amici is complemented by their signature Bloody Mary cart. A server rolls the cart tableside, and custom mixes your Bloody Mary. They start with house-infused pepper vodka, and build with all the standards: tomato juice, clamato, red pepper, horseradish, and the like.

On the other side of brunch, the *Worthington Inn* is steeped in tradition. You'll find the Inn at the center of Olde Worthington, in a building that dates back to 1831. The old three-story house originally served as a stagecoach stop and a hotel, all the while operating as a restaurant. (It's actually a few months shy of tying The Jury Room downtown for oldest continually operating restaurant in Columbus.) The rooms of Worthington Inn are cozy and ornately decorated. Eating brunch there feels a little bit like stepping back in time. On Saturdays, Chef Tom Smith and his crew prepare a farmers market brunch, complete with brunch items like buckwheat crepes and smoked salmon bagels; it's perfect for eating out on the front porch during busy market days. But the real feature of Worthington Inn is their Sunday brunch, which is often voted the best in town. This expansive buffet includes trays of eggs benedict, bacon and sausage, and chicken, plus a platter of shrimp and smoked salmon. You can also swing by the waffle and omelet bar, or eat slices of prime rib. Don't forget the dessert table, too!

If you want to visit:

DUE AMICI
67 East Gay Street
Columbus, OH 43215
(614) 224-9373
due-amici.com
@dueamici

WORTHINGTON INN
649 High Street
Worthington, OH 43085
(614) 885-2600
worthingtoninn.com
@worthingtoninn

Other brunches on this list are scattered around the city and range from nice chain restaurants to local taverns, from upscale dining establishments to some of the city's most respected eateries. Many feature the standard brunch fare: eggs benedicts, breakfast platters, steak and eggs, seafood, and Bloody Marys, but you'll find some more creative dishes in there, too.

BRIO TUSCAN GRILLE
3993 Easton Station
Columbus, OH 43219
(614) 416-4745
brioitalian.com
@brioitalian

1500 Polaris Pkwy #200
Columbus, OH 43240
(614) 410-0310
Brio is a national chain of Italian-themed restaurants, decorated like a wide open Tuscan villa. You can find Columbus' two locations in our major shopping centers at Easton and Polaris. The weekend brunch menu includes such delectables as white chocolate raspberry French toast, crab and shrimp crepes, and spinach and mushroom strata.

CAP CITY FINE DINER AND BAR
1299 Olentangy River Road
Columbus, OH 43212
(614) 291-3663
capcityfinediner.com

1301 Stoneridge Drive
Gahanna, OH 43230
(614) 478-9999
As mainstays of the Cameron Mitchell Restaurants, the two Cap City Diners serve comfort food classics in a slightly upscale atmosphere. Brunch ranges from flatbreads and wings, to steak and eggs, breakfast burritos, and four egg omelets.

J. LIU
50 West Bridge Street
Dublin, OH 43017
(614) 718-1818
jliurestaurant.com
@jliurestaurant

6880 North High Street
Worthington, OH 43085
(614) 888-1818
Jason Liu owns two restaurants in Columbus - one in Dublin and one in Worthington - that serve elegant Sunday brunch buffets. Sample many of the restaurants' Asian and Italian standards like sesame chicken, pad thai, or chicken Milanese. Or go the breakfast route with custom-made omelets and carved prime rib.

LINDEY'S
169 East Beck Street
Columbus, OH 43206
(614) 228-4343
lindeys.com
@lindeys
As one of Columbus' continually top-rated restaurants, Lindey's offers one of the more elegant brunches in town. The beautiful German Village location hosts customers in the dining room or out on the patio. Enjoy a brunch of rich salads, house-made pasta, or favorites like quiche, croque madame, and stuffed French toast.

MATT THE MILLER'S TAVERN
6725 Avery-Muirfield Drive
Dublin, OH 43016
(614) 799-9100
mtmtavern.com
@mattthemillers

1400 Grandview Avenue
Columbus, OH 43212
(614) 754-1026

Matt the Miller's Tavern is a newer edition to the Columbus brunching scene, but the comfy watering holes are drawing in loyal customers already. Sunday brunch buffets include everything from pasta to waffles to an omelet station. Diners can also try the make-your-own Bloody Mary bar. Let the bartender pour your vodka, and then customize your drink with tomato juice, lemon, celery, pickles, and spices.

94TH AERO SQUADRON
5030 Sawyer Road
Columbus, OH 43219
(614) 237-8887
94thaero.com

The 94th Aero Squadron offers a nice view of planes taking off and landing on the northeast side of Port Columbus International Airport. You can watch the planes while eating Sunday brunch. Sample everything from breads and desserts, to fajitas and stir-fries, to carved roast beef and biscuits with country gravy.

POLARIS GRILL
1835 Polaris Parkway
Columbus, OH 43240
(614) 431-5598
polarisgrill.com

Off Polaris Parkway in northern Columbus, the Polaris Grill has been serving up lunch, dinner, and brunch since 1997. In addition to catering and hosting banquet brunches, Polaris Grill offers a regular brunch at the restaurant. Try the range from green eggs and ham, wild berry waffles, a huge selection of benedicts, and a menu of Bloody Marys.

SAGE AMERICAN BISTRO
2653 North High Street
Columbus, OH 43202
(614) 267-7243
sageamericanbistro.com

It's easy to miss Sage's small storefront in Old North Columbus, but that tiny, brick-walled space serves one of Columbus' highest-rated Sunday brunches. Split a pitcher of mimosas or sip a cup of coffee while you enjoy fried eggs and johnny cakes, creme brulee French toast, or smoked turkey sandwiches. Or go for the Sage Benedict, which pairs poached eggs with duck confit, spinach, red peppers, and sage hollandaise on brioche bread.

SPAGIO
1295 Grandview Avenue
Columbus, OH 43212
(614) 486-1114
spagio.com
@spagiograndview

At over thirty years in service, Spagio and its adjoining wine bar anchor the "downtown" stretch of Grandview Avenue, along with Stauf's Coffee and Jeni's Ice Cream. Sit out on their patio or in the colorful dining room for your weekend brunch. Spagio serves up unique brunch items like the brunch calzone, stuffed French toast made with butter croissants, and potato cakes served with smoked salmon.

THIRD AND HOLLYWOOD
1433 West Third Avenue
Columbus, OH 43212
(614) 488-0303
thirdandhollywood.com

Created by the same team that owns Northstar Cafe, Third and Hollywood is named after its intersection in Grandview. The small weekend brunch menu includes blueberry scones, basil pesto omelets, chorizo and eggs, and French toast made with bananas, hazelnuts, and Nutella.

SOUTHEAST

GERMAN VILLAGE, OLDE TOWNE EAST, EAST SIDE, GAHANNA, & BEXLEY

Like every corner of the city, the Southeast side of Columbus features a diverse mix of neighborhoods and eateries. In this side of town, you can find delicious soul food joints serving comfort classics from down south. Venture further east to Bexley and Gahanna for neighborhoods alive with their heritage and proud of the little niches they've created. The southeast corner of Columbus also includes historic neighborhoods like German Village and Olde Towne East. In and amongst their brick streets are bakeries and diners, some of which have been cranking out inexpensive breakfasts for decades. Most importantly, on this side of town you can find a number of families who have pursued their culinary passions together and welcome their customers warmly every morning.

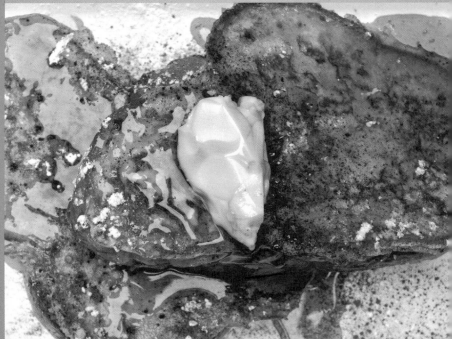

BLOCK'S BAGELS, DELI, & CAFE

3415 East Broad Street
Columbus, OH 43213

(614) 235-2551

blocksbagelsdeli.com

The Block family is a true New York family. Harold Block, the father, was born and raised on Coney Island. Audrey Block, his wife, was from Brooklyn. The family was living in Flushing, Queens, when Harold followed a job opportunity selling children's clothing in Columbus in 1961. It was a big move: they were the first of their families to leave the state of New York. Fortunately for Columbus, they brought a little bit of New York with them.

After the Blocks had lived in Columbus for several years, some family friends visited from New York and commented on the lack of New York water bagels in town. These friends owned bagel shops back in New York, and they encouraged the Blocks to start their own bakery to fill the niche in Columbus dining. So in 1967, they did.

> "Sit with Steve Block in one of his delis for even five minutes, and watch how many people he greets as they stop in."

New York water bagels are boiled first in water, before being baked in the oven. This process gives the bagel its unique shape, color, and crust (and it takes out a few calories, too). Block's is one of the very few bakeries in town that does it, or least does it on such a large scale. Their bagels are also certified kosher.

Block's Hot Bagels started small, in a 1000 square foot cafe on Columbus' east side. They served seven varieties of bagels. As Steve tells it, their specific type of bagels took about five years to catch on, and then the business took off. They began making more types of bagels and wholesaling them around town. In 1980 they opened a second location in

Reynoldsburg that allowed them to produce greater amounts. Seven years later, they moved their original location to a spot on East Broad Street.

Steve Block was 10 when his family's store opened, and he's now taken the reins. Both locations have expanded to include breakfast and lunch. In addition to the dozens of types of bagels (made almost around the clock at the Reynoldsburg location), Steve and his employees serve challah French toast and bagel sandwiches with lox, kosher salami, corned beef, and eggs. He attributes the family's success to dedicated employees, a consistent product that people like, a hardworking family, and, most importantly, the relationships he's made with his customers. The significance of those relationships is apparent: sit with him in one of the delis for even five minutes, and watch how many people he greets as they stop in.

If you can't make it out to one of Block's cafes, don't worry. Their bagels are sold all around the city by discerning restaurants and vendors.

CAFE CREEKSIDE

53 Granville Street
Gahanna, OH 43230

(614) 337-1819

The site of Gahanna's Cafe Creekside is perhaps the most storied of any restaurant in Columbus. The pictures on the diner's east wall share the ups and downs of nearly two centuries in business. The site has been some sort of eatery since 1823, when it opened as the Riverside Tavern. The original building lasted as a stage coach stop with a brothel upstairs, then over the years served as a bar and restaurant. In the mid-twentieth century, part of the building was damaged when a car ran into it; you can see pictures of the accident on the wall. At other times, the building served as a motorcycle shop with a bar named Signatures upstairs. About twenty years ago, however, that all changed when a fire burnt the two-story building to the ground. All that remains of the original structure is the basement, still made with beams and bricks. The

"Customers often request specials and dishes for the next day's menu."

building was reconstructed with three stories, and a restaurant once again opened along the creek, this time as the Creekside Grill. Finally, about a decade ago, a new owner renamed the eatery Cafe Creekside, and the restaurant you can visit today took shape.

The building itself is still alive with history. Plaques and pictures tell the story, and over the years, the decorations have remained mostly the same. Wood accents surround red booths and stools at the counter. Regulars chat with each other and their servers, as they have for years.

Owner Chris Katanyuta has been in charge of the restaurant for roughly four years, and she maintains tradition using her vast experience in the restaurant industry. She started cooking when she was 14, easily found her way into the business, and has worked everywhere from big hotels to mom-and-pop operations, from exclusive eateries with

Columbus' best known chefs to corporate chains. Everything but fast food, she says. While working for the First Watch restaurant chain, she got into breakfast. Her passion drove her to find work at a locally-owned restaurant, and she ended up at Cafe Creekside. She worked as a regular employee, then took ownership three years later.

She's focused on her efforts on whipping up big comfort food breakfasts and building close relationships with her clientele. Customers often request specials and dishes for the next day's menu. When Chris' regulars come in with a cold, she fixes up a fresh batch of chicken broth. Whenever she makes her chicken tortilla soup, Chris always saves a bowl without cilantro for one customer.

Cafe Creekside serves all of your breakfast standards: creamed chipped beef, corned beef hash, breakfast burritos, frittatas, and platters like the Working Man's Breakfast that combine everything. Load up with a Belgian waffle, French toast, or buttermilk and multigrain pancakes. Chris' eggs benedict, with Canadian bacon, poached eggs, English muffins, and fresh hollandaise, is always a hit. All of her breakfasts invite you to grab a seat at the counter, become a regular, and take part in Cafe Creekside's long history.

CREOLE KITCHEN

1052 Mount Vernon Avenue
Columbus, OH 43203

(614) 372-3333

creolekitchen.biz

BREAKFAST

HOT BISCUIT WITH BUTTER AND JAM	$ 1.00
BEIGNETS AND ASSORTED PASTRIES	
PANCAKES	$ 4.00
MAPLE SYRUP AND BUTTER	
BREAKFAST SANDWICH ON A BISCUIT	$ 3.50
EGG, HAM, SAUSAGE, BACON, CHEESE	
EGGS BASIN STREET ON RICE PATTIES	
WITH RED BEANS & ANDOUILLE SAUSAGE	
POACHED EGGS, BEARNISE SAUCE	$ 5.00
CREOLE EGGS BENEDICT ON A BISCUIT	
HAM, POACH EGGS, BEARNISE SAUCE	
HOME FRIES OR GRITS	$ 5.00

OMELETS
SERVED WITH GRITS, CHEESE GRITS OR HOME FRIES

CREOLE OMELET - ANDOUILLE SAUSAGE, TASSO HAM ONION, TOMATO, CHEESE	$ 5.00
MUSHROOM OMELET - ONION, TOMATO, CHEESE	$ 5.00
EGGS SCRAMBLE OR OVERLIGHT	
WITH SAUSAGE, BACON OR HAM	$ 5.00
HAM WITH RED EYE GRAVY OVER GRITS	
BEEF GRILLADES	
BEEF BRAISED IN A SAUCE OF ONIONS, GREEN PEPPERS, CELERY, TOMATOES AND GARLIC OVER GRITS	

SALADS

	$ 4.00	CHEF SALAD	$ 4.00
...NED SALMON			
	$ 2.00	TOSS SALAD	$ 2.00

In the first two years in business, Chef Henry Butcher had a lot of explaining to do. He introduced Columbus to honest Louisiana Creole cooking. Columbus customers just didn't know Creole cooking, so he made it a mission to familiarize them with the flavors, ingredients, and recipes from his childhood.

Two things make his restaurant work: love and discipline. He learned the love at an early age, "tied to his grandmother's apron strings" growing up. He spent time in the kitchen with her in rural Louisiana, learning the basics while using produce and meats from the family farm. Over the years he began working in restaurants in New Orleans, until his family - including eight brothers and two sisters - moved up to Columbus. It was in Columbus that he learned the discipline in his cooking, especially from an Italian chef named Chef Caruso. Over the years, he traveled to culinary school in New York, then worked as a sous chef for various Hyatt Hotel locations, and returned to Columbus to spend his time at institutions like the now-gone Ollie's Grandview, mainstay Tony's Ristorante, and eventually the Delaware Hotel. The hotel closed after Chef Butcher spent thirteen years cooking there, and about that time, he formulated the plan for his own restaurant; Creole Kitchen opened its doors in 2006.

"In Chef Butcher's kitchen, you'll find dishes that you can't find anywhere else in Columbus."

Creole Kitchen does primarily take-out - and a LOT of it, judging by the crowd. The phone starts ringing promptly at 7 a.m. Recently, Chef Butcher added a few small tables to give you the chance to sit and watch him at work. It's there that he shares his love of cooking. The open kitchen lets you watch the busy crew as they whip up fresh béarnaise

sauce, stir pots of grits, fry beignets, and flip creole omelets. The feeling is much like being invited to his grandmother's kitchen, where the process is part of the entertainment, while you enjoy the relationships built over food. Chef Butcher values those relationships, gathering a dedicated crew of workers around him. And if you're lucky, you may glimpse the chef's two daughters or his son in the restaurant, too.

In Chef Butcher's kitchen, you'll find dishes that you can't find anywhere else in Columbus. For a sweet starter, try the beignets, small fried dough balls tossed in powdered sugar. Another popular

dish is the Eggs Basin Street, what Chef Butcher calls the "original creole benedict," poached eggs served over a bed of red bean cakes, rice, and andouille sausage, and topped with béarnaise sauce. (Béarnaise is a form of hollandaise that uses vinegar and tarragon as its base, rather than lemon juice.) Other Kitchen favorites include the Beef Grillade, steak simmered in a sauce of onions, garlic, tomatoes, and green peppers, served over grits. Whatever you order, the food is honest and unique, seasoned with Chef Butcher's own blend, which he calls his "mojo."

GERMAN VILLAGE COFFEE SHOP

193 Thurman Avenue
Columbus, OH 43206

(614) 443-8900

gvcoffeeshop.com

@gvcoffeeshop

Partners Craig Burke and Christa Foreman have known each other since they were seven years old, growing up in Warren, Ohio, going to high school and college together, and eventually moving together to Columbus as a stop before they headed out to big city life in New York or Chicago. They soon found themselves calling Columbus home, both finding jobs in corporate America. In establishing their lives here, they became regulars at the German Village Coffee Shop. When the restaurant was put up for sale in 2003, they decided - despite a collective zero years experience in the restaurant business - to take a chance and buy it.

In buying the Coffee Shop, Craig and Christa took over a long and storied history. The location opened in 1953 as a lunch counter called Laff's Lunch. You can see all sorts of black and white photos of Laff's plastering the walls above your booth. It remained that way until 1981, when a new owner renamed it to the German Village Coffee Shop. Over the years, subsequent owners changed very little about the restaurant, with no reason to, as very loyal (and vocal) customers continued filling the booths and stools for their favorite omelets, hash browns, and buttery French toast.

"The regulars visit once or even twice a day, not to mention every weekend."

German Village Coffee Shop is the quintessential example of the neighborhood diner. The regulars visit once or even twice a day, not to mention every weekend. They know Craig and Christa. They ask about each other's families. They notice when Craig takes a day off. They even built some of the restaurant itself: the signature wooden shelves holding loaves of bread, and the wooden table caddies with salt, pepper, and napkins above each booth were assembled by a customer named Gene.

The interior is dim, noisy, and almost always packed full of regulars. Open the door too wide and you may bump someone waiting for their spot at the counter. Aside from a single fluorescent light in the middle of the space, the only other lights are small lamps hung above each booth.

With the signature diner experience, the Coffee Shop serves up the signature diner menu. Their sign out front says they are "Home of the Western Omelette," a monster dish of eggs folded over ham, cheese, tomatoes, mushrooms, onions, and green peppers. Each of the regulars claims their own favorites, but the Shop is also known for their hash browns covered in onions and cheese, pancakes stacked high, and their extra crispy bacon pressed out on the grill.

SKILLET

410 East Whittier Street
Columbus, OH 43206

(614) 443-2266

skilletruf.com

@skilletruf

Even in its early stages, Skillet drew a lot of attention to itself. Occupying the original space of Banana Bean Cafe, they opened in November 2009 with a little bit of fanfare, but quickly became a favorite for seasoned foodies and general German Village locals alike. The restaurant began as an idea for a food truck from Patrick Caskey. He and

sweet potato hash, mixing duck meat with sweet potatoes and covering it with fresh greens and a hearty fried duck egg.

The menu shifts with the seasons; they're reprinted every weekend based on what local farms produce. The restaurant is clearly a hit: they've received

"The combination of breakfast mainstays plus creative preparation of local goods in a neighborhood eatery led to the restaurant's subtitle of "rustic. urban. food.""

his father were working at the Banana Bean Cafe, which had moved west into the Brewery District. With the 30-seat space available on Whittier Street, they took over to start Skillet as a brick-and-mortar operation first. (Their food truck can now be found in warmer months around town, too!)

Father and son Kevin and Patrick Caskey, the dynamic duo in the kitchen, made a mark by taking breakfast signatures like oatmeal, omelets, hash, and French toast and putting their own funky spin on it. (Wife and mother Angela hides in the kitchen and away from the cameras, but she's as much a part of this, too! Watch for her hand in the kitchen, as well.) They draw on surrounding Ohio farmland to supply their kitchen with eggs, meats, cheese, breads, fruits, and vegetables. The combination of breakfast mainstays plus creative preparation of local goods in a neighborhood eatery led to the restaurant's subtitle of "rustic. urban. food."

Cases in point: in the autumn you can find Kevin's famous take on a hearty oatmeal: he makes a breakfast risotto topped with seared apples, a bourbon/molasses gravy, and mascarpone cheese. Or you can try the breakfast poutine, their version of a Canadian comfort food with fingerling potatoes, cheese curds, poached eggs, and a spicy/smokey tasso gravy. They've also done a duck and

multiple features in local and regional publications, as well as a spot on a national PBS special. Dedicated brunchers fill up the restaurant shortly after opening every Saturday and Sunday.

EXTRA HELPINGS

THE ANGRY BAKER

891 Oak Street
Columbus, OH 43205
(614) 947-0976
theangrybakerote.com
@theangrybaker

A slick new bakery on a burgeoning corner of Olde Towne East featuring baked goods like toasted brioche rolls, sweet and savory scones, and Dr. Pepper cake. They've also got coffee and creative sandwiches like smoked salmon on a croissant, or a French toast sandwich with ham, Swiss, and maple syrup. Rotating vegan options are available, too!

BEXLEY COFFEE SHOP

492 North Cassady Avenue
Columbus, OH 43209
(614) 253-3788
thebexleycoffeeshop.com

A small coffee shop roasting their own beans and offering basic tea service. Nibble on goods made by local companies like Pattycake and Sassafras Bakeries, enjoy some toasted Sammy's Bagels, or try biscotti and jam made in the neighborhood.

THE CLARMONT

684 South High Street
Columbus, OH 43215
(614) 443-1125
clarmontrestaurant.com
@theclarmont

A downtown dining institution since 1947, The Clarmont serves breakfast six days a week. A delightful art deco style, rose lamps, and pastel colors provide the mood for breakfast standards like pan-fried corned beef hash and fresh-squeezed orange juice. Here you can also try some harder-to-find dishes like fried chicken livers and eggs benedict with smoked salmon.

CRAZY GOAT COFFEE

505 Creekside Plaza
Gahanna, OH 43230
(614) 285-4628
crazygoatcoffee.com
@crazygoatcoffee

In Gahanna's Creekside neighborhood, this little coffee shop is named after the legend that an Ethiopian goatherder discovered coffee when his goats behaved erratically after eating the berries. Crazy Goat is the only Columbus-area coffee shop to serve Chicago-made Intelligensia coffee. Enjoy your coffee while snacking on bagels, baked goods, quiche, or parfaits.

EASY STREET CAFE

197 Thurman Avenue
Columbus, OH 43206
(614) 444-3279
theeasystreetcafe.com

Located on Thurman Street in German Village, Easy Street mixes traditional American and Greek breakfasts. Visit during the week or for a weekend brunch of omelets, pancakes (including Reese's Pieces pancakes!), plus special breakfast pitas, all in an eclectic environment packed with signs, posters, and neon lights.

FIRST WATCH

496 South High Street
Columbus, Oh 43215
(614) 228-7554
firstwatch.com
@firstwatch

The German Village location of this breakfast chain is a favorite with the business crowd, what with its proximity to downtown. Decorated in cool retirement community colors, this casual cafe offers light and healthy versions of breakfast foods, like the Bacado

BREAKFAST IN PICKERINGTON

If you're up for a little driving before breakfast, you can always head east out of Columbus to the little town of Pickerington. The city lies about twenty minutes from downtown Columbus, and there you can find a few good breakfasts to start your day. If you're in the mood for something traditional, stop into the little *Old Village Diner*. There you'll find the classic diner breakfast in big portions and for low prices. Try French toast, omelets, breakfast sandwiches, or the 2x2x2: two pancakes, two eggs, and two servings of meat. For something a little different than the old diner breakfast, you need to stop by the newer *Village Crepe*. Owner Wayne Moore opened the shop in 2010 after years of making crepes for his kids at home. He serves omelets, frittatas, French toast, and the classics, too, but the real feature are his Parisian-style crepes. You can try sweet crepes filled with cream cheese, hazelnut spread, or homemade preserves, or go for the savory selection, with ingredients like ricotta and spinach or ham and asparagus. He also rotates different special crepes each week. If it's some caffeine and to-go breakfast you're looking for, you can head north of the town center to *Planet Coffee & Tea Company*. They can serve or deliver espresso, cappuccinos, and hot cocoa, prepare frappes and smoothies, or even whip up baked goods and breakfast burritos.

Omelet, with bacon, avocado, and cheese. Or you can try the Mexican-themed dishes, like a Chickichanga: whipped eggs, spicy chicken and chorizo, plus cheese, veggies, and a verde sauce wrapped in a tortilla.

FRANK'S RESTAURANT
2932 East Broad Street
Columbus, OH 43209
(614) 236-1959

A tiny, inexpensive diner serving breakfast all day, with a daily specials menu that rotates pancakes, omelets, sausage gravy, home fries, and sandwiches. Most breakfast dishes run in the $3-6 range, and will fill you up.

GOLDEN DONUTS & DINER
1928 Lockbourne Road
Columbus, OH 43207
(614) 443-1766

An old school South Side donut joint, with one of those old neon signs that are disappearing from the American landscape. Serving all the basic breakfast items, like steak and eggs, home fries, and pancakes, plus lots of fresh donuts: honey dipped, cinnamon, cake, and apple fritters.

GRILL & SKILLET DINER
2924 East Main Street
Columbus, OH 43209
(614) 231-1702

This little Main Street diner is another one of those old time spots that's been around for decades and serves breakfast classics all day. Sit at the counter or slide into a booth for a Frenchy's Breakfast Sandwich, a croissant stuffed with eggs, meat and cheese. Try omelets filled with chili or corned beef hash, or big favorites like smothered potatoes, buttermilk pancakes, or steak and eggs. Wash it all down with good old diner coffee.

JOLLY PIRATE DONUTS
3923 East Broad Street
Columbus, OH 43213
(614) 231-7556

One of the remaining locations of a central Ohio chain of donut shops, and one of three around Columbus. Let the yellow neon sign guide you to their full range of fresh donuts made in-house. Crews at Jolly Pirate make about forty-five different types of donuts, in addition to serving coffee, juices, and tea.

KATZINGER'S DELICATESSEN

475 South Third Street
Columbus, OH 43215
(614) 228-3354
katzingers.com
@katzingers

Easily Columbus' most recognizable deli, Katzinger's has been featured repeatedly on cable television food shows for their huge sandwiches, deli meats, and Jewish specialties. But they can also teach you how delis do breakfast. Try one of their bagels, some cheese blintzes, Eric's corned beef hash, or deli sandwiches loaded with egg salad, smoked salmon, or whitefish fillets.

LALIBELA RESTAURANT & BAR

1111 South Hamilton Road
Columbus, OH 43227
(614) 235-5355

This southeast side restaurant opens daily to serve an authentic Ethiopian breakfast. Ethiopian food is typically served with *injera*, a spongy, tangy bread used to scoop up bites of your meal. Dishes include versions of *firfir*, a sweet version mixes injera with yogurt, while a savory version cooks the bread with beef stew. Another mainstay of the Ethiopian breakfast is *fuul*, versions of which combine crushed fava beans with eggs, meat, and vegetables, or even one with peanut butter, olive oil, and veggies. Try mango juice, tea, or coffee along with your meal.

PISTACIA VERA

541 South Third Street
Columbus, OH 43215
(614) 220-9070
pistaciavera.com

Perhaps Columbus' best patisserie, Pistacia Vera serves coffee, tea, and gorgeous baked goods like croissants, pinwheels, bearclaws, and caneles. Their daily brunch menu includes items like Croque Monsieur, a baked dish of local ham, cheese, and a delicate white sauce over brioche. You can also order Shirred Eggs: baked eggs served over ratatouille and parmigiano reggiano. Bring a camera on your visit: Pistacia Vera is also one of Columbus' most sparkling photogenic food stops.

PLANK'S CAFE & PIZZERIA

743 Parsons Avenue
Columbus, OH 43206
(614) 443-6251
plankscafe.com

Breakfast at a pizza place? That's right. The fact that Plank's Cafe, a long-time German Village institution, offers breakfast is a great example of hidden gems of Columbus. Who would have thought a place known for their pizza also churns out French toast, omelets, or grilled breakfast sandwiches?

PORTICO

85 Parsons Avenue
Columbus, OH 43205
(614) 744-0101

Portico is your one-stop shop on Parsons Avenue. Pick up local coffee or bagels, breakfast sandwiches, quiche, or homemade coffee cake. Big windows offer a chance to sit and nibble, or park nearby for a quick stop on the go.

RESCH'S BAKERY

4061 East Livingston Avenue
Columbus, OH 43227
(614) 237-7421

Celebrating its 100th anniversary in 2012, Resch's is an old school German bakery complete with little old ladies behind the counter. A bright mural of Mr. Resch's mother's hometown of Mittlenberg, Germany is the only splash of color amongst wooden shelves lining the room. Watch the steady stream of customers line up for boxes of fresh donuts, breads, and granny rolls (a vanilla iced cinnamon roll topped with chopped walnuts).

SMOTHERED GRAVY

1114 East Main Street
Columbus, OH 43205
(614) 252-3202

A soul food joint long in the making. While you enjoy chicken and waffles, catfish nuggets, shrimp and grits, or salmon cakes, ask owner Eugena Dade to tell you her story. She comes from a long line of skilled cooks and restaurant owners, and her eatery stands as a piece of living history in homage to her family's love of community and cooking.

TEE JAYE'S COUNTRY PLACE

1385 Parsons Avenue
Columbus, OH 43206
(614) 444-6291
barnyardbuster.com
@teejayes

350 South Hamilton Road
Columbus, OH 43213
(614) 861-4160

Two Tee Jaye's locations serve this corner of Columbus, including the original on Parsons Avenue. A local chain of "down home cooking" family restaurants, Tee Jaye's got its start in late 1970 by Jules and Nita Sokol. After ill health forced him to quit running a chain of twenty-eight Beverlee Drive-Ins around Ohio, Jules started TeeJaye's, which just recently celebrated 40 years of serving Barnyard Busters, cornmeal pancakes, and creamed chipped beef.

UPPER CUP COFFEE

79 Parsons Avenue
Columbus, OH 43205
(614) 235-5600
myuppercupcoffee.com

A new addition to Olde Towne East, Upper Cup roasts their own beans and offers simple coffee, tea, and espresso. Grab your coffee on the go, or stop an enjoy the coffee-roasting smell at one of their small tables.

URBAN SPIRIT COFFEE SHOP

893 East Long Street
Columbus, OH 43203
(614) 253-7778
urban-spirit.com
@urbanspiritcafe

Urban Spirit celebrates its location and heritage, in the center of Columbus' former jazz district, with coffee drinks, smoothies, and snacks named after jazz greats. Try a Coletrane smoothie or a Lady Ella amaretto latte. While there, enjoy the art gallery or stay late for a poetry slam.

WINANS FINE CHOCOLATES & COFFEES

897 South Third Street
Columbus, OH 43206
(614) 445-6464
winanscolumbus.com
@winanscolumbus

Winans has been producing chocolates and roasted coffee since the late 1800's in Piqua, Ohio, and just recently opened a shop in German Village. In addition to sampling their chocolate, brittle, and nuts, you can try Sumatra or Costa Rican coffee, or flavored vanilla cream or creme brulee roasts.

ZANZIBAR BREWS

740 East Long Street
Columbus, OH 43203
(614) 758-0111
zanzibarbrews.com
@zanzibarbrews

A new coffee shop in the King-Lincoln District, across the street from the newly-renovated Lincoln Theatre, with plenty of room for meetings and studying. Grab an espresso made with Stauf's roasts or a plate of eggs, meat, and hash browns in the morning. You can also create your own breakfast sandwich using wraps, bread, English muffins, or bagels.

ZENCHA TEA SALON

2396 East Main Street
Columbus, OH 43209
(614) 237-9690
zen-cha.com
@zenchateasalon

ZenCha's second location opened in Bexley in 2011, and offers the same complete range of teas from around the world, all served to exacting standards. Enjoy your tea in a quiet, relaxing atmosphere, along with a weekend brunch menu of quiche, eggs in a basket, or sweet and savory pancakes and waffles, all made with tea in the batter.